LIVING IN HOPE AND HISTORY

NOTES FROM OUR CENTURY

Nadine Gordimer

BLOOMSBURY

First published in Great Britain 1999
This paperback edition published 2000

Copyright © 1999 by Felix Licensing, B.V.

The moral right of the author has been asserted

Bloomsbury Publishing Plc, 38 Soho Square, London W1V 5DF

A CIP catalogue record for this book
is available from the British Library

ISBN 0 7475 4823 4

Printed in Great Britain by Clays Ltd, St Ives plc

For Antonin Miguet and Conrad Cassirer
The new century is theirs

CONTENTS

One of the things a writer is for is to say the unsayable,
to speak the unspeakable, to ask difficult questions.
—Salman Rushdie

How shall we look at each other then?
—Mongane Wally Serote

The ceaseless adventure.

—Jawaharlal Nehru

History says, Don't hope
On this side of the grave,
But then, once in a lifetime
The longed-for tidal wave
Of justice can rise up,
And hope and history rhyme.
                    —*Seamus Heaney*

One of the things a writer is for is to say the unsayable, to

speak the unspeakable, to ask difficult questions.

—Salman Rushdie

THREE IN A BED:

FICTION, MORALS, AND POLITICS

T hree in a bed: it's a kinky cultural affair. I had better
identify the partners.

Politics and morals, as concepts, need no introduction, although their relationship is shadily ambiguous. But fiction has defining responsibilities that I shall be questioning all
through what I have to say, so I shall begin right away with the
basic, dictionary definition of what fiction is supposed to be.

Fiction, says the *Oxford English Dictionary*, is 'the action of
feigning or inventing imaginary existences, events, states of
things . . . prose novels and stories collectively'. So poetry,
according to the OED, is not fiction. The more I ponder this,
the more it amazes me; the more I challenge it. Does the poet
not invent imaginary existences, events, states of things?

If I should ask any erudite and literary gathering to give
examples of the powers of the poets' invention of imaginary
existences, events, the poets' matchless evocation of 'states of

things', all drawn, just as the prose writers' is, from life—the fact of life—as the genie is smoked from the bottle, I could fill pages with quotations. If fiction is the suprareal spirit of the imagination, then poetry is the ultimate fiction. In speaking of fiction, I should be understood to be including poetry.

What is politics doing in bed with fiction? Morals have bedded with story-telling since the magic of the imaginative capacity developed in the human brain—and in my ignorance of a scientific explanation of changes in the cerebrum or whatever, to account for this faculty, I believe it was the inkling development that here was somewhere where the truth about being alive might lie. The harsh lessons of daily existence, coexistence between human and human, with animals and nature, could be made sense of in the ordering of properties by the transforming imagination, working upon the 'states of things'. With this faculty fully developed, great art in fiction can evolve in imaginative revelation to fit the crises of an age that comes after its own, undreamt of when it was written. *Moby-Dick* can now be seen as an allegory of environmental tragedy. 'The whale is the agent of cosmic retribution': we have sought to destroy the splendid creature that is nature, believing we could survive only by 'winning' a battle against nature; now we see our death in the death of nature, brought about by ourselves.

But the first result of the faculty of the imagination was, of course, religion. And from the gods (what a supreme feat of the imagination they were!), establishing a divine order out of the unseen, came the secular, down-to-soil-and-toil order of morals, so that humans could somehow live together, and in balance with other creatures.

Morals are the husband/wife of fiction. And politics? Politics somehow followed morals in, picking the lock and immobilizing the alarm system. At first it was in the dark, perhaps, and fiction thought the embrace of politics was that of morals, didn't know the difference . . . And this is understandable. Morals and politics have a family connection. Politics' ancestry is morality—way back, and generally accepted as forgotten. The resemblance is faded. In the light of morning, if fiction accepts the third presence within the sheets it is soon in full cognisance of who and what politics is.

Let me not carry my allegory too far. Just one generation further. From this kinky situation came two offspring, Conformity and Commitment. And you will know who fathered whom.

Until 1988 I would have said that the pressures to write fiction that would conform to a specific *morality*, whether secular or religious, long had been, could be, and were, safely ignored by writers in modern times. The Vatican still has its list of proscribed works, but in most countries one assumed there was freedom of expression—so far as religion was concerned. (The exception was perhaps in certain North American schools . . .)

Blasphemy? A quaint taboo, outdated, like the dashes which used to appear between the first and last letters of four-letter words. Where censorship was rigidly practised, in Eastern Europe, the Soviet Union, and South Africa, for example, the censors were concerned with what was considered politically subversive in literature, not with what might offend or subvert religious sensibilities. (In the Soviet Union these were not recognized, anyway.) This was true even in South Africa, where the Dutch Reformed Church with a particular form of Calvinistic prudery had twisted religion to the service of racism and identified the church with the security of the state, including its sexual morality based on the supposed "purity" of one race. A decade ago, in 1988, an actor in South Africa could not get away with exclaiming "My God!" in a secular context on the stage, and *Jesus Christ Superstar* was banned; by 1989, savage satire of the church and its morality was ignored. As for sexual permissiveness, full frontal nudity in films was not snipped by the censor's scissors.

But in holding this illusion about freedom of expression in terms of religious and sexual morality, I was falling into the ignorance Islam finds reprehensible in the Judeo-Christian-atheist world (more strange bedfellows)—that world's ignorance of the absolute conformity to religious taboos that is sacred to Islam. And here Islam was right; I should have known that this kind of censorship was not evolving into tolerance, least of the rights of non-Muslim countries to grant their citizens the freedom of disbelief, but was instead becoming an international gale force of growing religious fanaticism. Then came the holy war against *The Satanic Verses*, in which the enemy was a single fiction, a single writer, and the might and money of the Islamic world were deployed in the *fatwa*: death to Salman Rushdie.

Now I, and other writers, were stunned to know that situations were back with us where religious persecution—the denial of people's right to follow their faith in freedom—is turned on its head, and religion *persecutes* freedom—not alone freedom of expression but a writer's freedom of movement, finally a writer's *right to life itself*. Now in a new decade, with freedoms rising, we see that while a writer becomes president in one country, another writer is being hounded to death throughout the world. We see how a religion has the power to terrorize, through its followers, across all frontiers. Political refugees from repressive regimes may seek asylum elsewhere; Salman Rushdie has nowhere to go. Islam's edict of death takes terrorist jurisdiction everywhere, contemptuous of the laws of any country.

Pre-Freudian hypocrisy, puritan prudery may be forgotten. The horror of what has happened to Rushdie is a hand fallen heavily on the shoulder of fiction: pressures to write in conformity with a specific morality still can arrive, and pursue with incredible vindictiveness, even if this is unlikely to happen to most writers.

Am I positing that morals should be divorced from fiction? That fiction is free of any moral obligation? No. Fiction's morality lies in taking the freedom to explore and examine contemporary morals, including moral systems such as religions, with unafraid honesty.

This has not been an easy relationship, whether in the ghastly extreme of Salman Rushdie's experience or, say, that of Gustave Flaubert, who, commenting on the indecency case against *Madame Bovary* after he won it in 1857, wrote of the establishment of spurious literary values and the devaluation of real literary values such a case implies for fiction. 'My book is going to sell unusually well . . . But I am infuriated when I think of the trial; it has deflected attention from the novel's artistic success . . . to such a point that all this row disquiets me profoundly . . . I long to . . . publish nothing; never to be talked of again.'

The relationship of fiction with politics has not had the kind of husband/fatherly authoritarian sanction that morals, with their religious origins, lingeringly have. No literary critic I know of suggests that *moralizing* as opposed to 'immorality' has no place in fiction, whereas many works of fiction are declared 'spoiled' by the writer's recognition of politics as as great a motivation of character as sex or religion. Of course, this lack of sanction is charactistic of an affair, a wild love affair in which great tensions arise, embraces and repulsions succeed one another, distress and celebration are confused, loyalty and betrayal change place, accusations fly. And whether the fiction writer gets involved with politics initially through his/her convictions as a citizen pushing, within, against the necessary detachment of the writer, or whether the involvement comes about through the pressure of seduction from without, the same problems in the relationship occur and have to be dealt with *in the fiction* as well as in the life.

For when have writers not lived in time of political conflict? Whose Golden Age, whose Belle Epoch, whose Roaring Twenties were these so-named lovely times?

The time of slave and peasant misery, while sculptors sought perfect proportions of the human torso? The time of revolutionaries in Czar Alexander's prisons, while Grand Dukes built mansions in Nice? The time of the hungry and unemployed, offered the salvation of growing Fascism while playboys and girls danced balancing glasses of pink champagne?

When, overtly or implicitly, could writers evade politics? Even those writers who have seen fiction as the pure exploration of language, as music is the exploration of sound, the babbling of Dada and the page-shuffling of Burroughs have been in reaction to what each revolted against in the politically-imposed spirit of their respective times; theirs were literary movements that were an act—however far-out—of acknowledgement of a relationship between politics and fiction.

It seems there is no getting away from the relationship. On the one hand, we live in what Seamus Heaney calls a world where the 'undirected play of the imagination is regarded at best as luxury or licentiousness, at worst as heresy or treason. In ideal republics . . . it is a common expectation that the writer will sign over his or her venturesome and potentially disruptive activity into the keeping of official doctrine, traditional system, a party line, whatever . . . ' Gerard Manley Hopkins felt obliged to abandon poetry when he entered the Jesuits 'as not having to do with my vocation'; a submission of the imagination to religious orthodoxy exactly comparable to that demanded of writers, in many instances in our time, by political orthodoxies.

We are shocked by such clear cases of creativity outlawed. But things are not always so drastically simple. Not every fiction writer entering a relation with politics trades imagination for the hair shirt of the party hack. There is also the case of the writer whose imaginative powers are genuinely roused by and involved with the spirit of politics as he or she personally experiences it. And it may not be the free choice of a Byron. It can be virtually inescapable in times and places of socially seismic upheaval. Society shakes, the walls of entities fall; the writer has known the evil, indifference, or cupidity of the old order, and the spirit of creativity naturally pushes towards new growth. The writer is moved to fashion an expression of a new order, accepted on trust as an advance in human freedom that therefore also will be the release of a greater creativity.

'Russia became a garden of nightingales. Poets sprang up as never before. People barely had the strength to live but they were all singing'—so wrote Andrey Bely in the early days of the Russian Revolution. And one of Pasternak's biographers, Peter Levi, notes that Pasternak—popularly known to the West, on the evidence of his disillusioned *Dr. Zhivago*, as *the* Russian anti-Communist writer—in his young days contributed manifestos to the 'infighting of the day'. In his poem to Stalin he sang:

> *We want the glorious. We want the good.*
> *We want to see things free from fear.*
> *Unlike some fancy fop, the spendthrift*
> *of his bright, brief span, we yearn*
> *for labour shared by everyone,*
> *for the common discipline of law.*

This yearning is addressed by writers in different ways, as fiction seeks a proper relation with politics. In the Soviet Union of Pasternak's day, some fell into what the Italian contemporary writer Claudio Magris, in a different context, calls with devastating cynicism, 'A sincere but perverted passion for freedom, which led . . . into mechanical servitude, as is the way with sin.' The noble passion deteriorated to the tragically shabby, as in the 1930s the Writers Union turned on itself to beat out all but mediocrity-mouthing platitudes, driving Mayakovsky to suicide and turning down Pasternak's plea to be granted a place where he would have somewhere other than a freezing partitioned slice of a room in which to write and live. Yet Pasternak had not abandoned belief—never did—in the original noble purpose of revolution. When Trotsky asked why he had begun to abstain from social themes, Pasternak wrote to a friend, 'I told him *My Sister, Life* [his then recent book] was revolutionary in the best sense of the word. That the phase of the revolution closest to the heart . . . the *morning* of the revolution, and its outburst when it returns man to the *nature* of man and looks at the state with the eyes of *natural* right.' But for Pasternak the writing of this period had become, by the edicts of the state and the Writers Union, 'a train derailed and lying at the bottom of an embankment'. And in this choice of an image there is a kind of desperate subconscious assertion of the creativity so threatened in himself and his fellow writers, since trains, in his era perhaps symbolic of the pace at which passes, fleetingly, the meaning of life the writer must catch, recur so often in his work.

Yeats's 'terrible beauty' of the historic moments when people seek a new order to 'return man to the nature of man, a state of natural right', does not always make politics the murderer of fiction. The Brechts and Nerudas survive, keeping that vision.

But the relation, like all vital ones, always implies some danger. The first dismaying discovery for the writer is once again best expressed by Magris's cynicism: 'The lie is quite as real as the truth, it works upon the world, transforms it'; whereas the fiction writer, in pursuit of truth beyond the guise of reasoning, has believed that truth, however elusive, is the only reality. Yet we have seen the lie transforming; we have had Goebbels. And his international descendents, practising that transformation on the people of a number of countries, including the white people of my own country, who accepted the lie that apartheid was both divinely decreed and secularly just, and created a society on its precepts.

To be aware that the lie also can transform the world places an enormous responsibility on art to counter this with its own transformations; the knowledge that the writer's searching and intuition gain instinctively contradicts the lie.

> *We page through each other's faces*
> *We read each looking eye . . .*
> *It has taken lives to be able to do so*

—writes the South African poet Mongane Wally Serote. We may refuse to write according to any orthodoxy, we may refuse to toe any party line, even that drawn by the cause we know to be just, and our own, but we cannot refuse the responsibility of what we know. What we know beyond surface reality has to become what—again in Serote's words—'We want the world to know'; we must in this, our inescapable relation with politics, 'page for wisdom through the stubborn night'.

At its crudest and most easily identifiable, the stubborn night is politically-inspired censorship, and yet, in some countries where no writer is locked up or his writings banned, and censorship is minimal and open to challenge by the law, fiction remains threatened by the power of the lie. Orwell alerted us to the insidious destruction of truth in the distortion of what words mean; but 1984 passed years ago, and he is remembered more for the cute cartoon movie of an *Animal Farm* than for a prophetic warning about the abuse of language. Harold Pinter spoke recently of 'a disease at the very centre of language, so that language becomes a permanent masquerade, a tapestry of lies. The ruthless and cynical mutilation and degradation of human beings, both in spirit and body . . . these actions are justified by rhetorical gambits, sterile terminology and concepts of power which stink. Are we ever going to look at the language we use, I wonder? Is it within our capabilities to do so? . . . Does reality essentially remain outside language, separate, obdurate, alien, not susceptible to description? Is an accurate and vital correspondence between what is and our perception of it impossible? Or is it that we are obliged to use language only in order to obscure and distort reality—to distort what *is*—to distort what *happens*— because we fear it? . . . I believe it's because of the way we use language that we have got ourselves into this terrible trap, where words like freedom, democracy and Christian values are still used to justify barbaric and shameful policies and acts.'

The writer has no reason to be if, for him or her, reality remains outside language. An accurate and vital correspondence between what is and the perception of the writer is what the fiction writer has to seek, finding the real meaning of words to express 'the states of things', shedding the ready-made concepts smuggled into language by politics.

All very fine in theory, yes—but how would you refer, in a novel, to the term 'final solution', coined by the Nazis; the term 'Bantustans', coined by a South African government in the sixties to disguise the dispossession of blacks of their citizenship rights and land; the term 'constructive engagement' coined by the government of the U.S.A. in the seventies in its foreign policy that evaded outright rejection of apartheid—how would you do this without paragraphs of explanation (which have no place in a novel) of what their counterfeits of reality actually were?

The false currency of meaning jingles conveniently in our vocabularies; but it is no small change. It becomes accepted values, for which writers bear responsibility. Every fiction writer has to struggle to expose them by discarding them, for the reader, in favour of the reality of the 'states of things', since generally journalism—supposed to be 'fact' as opposed to 'fiction'— won't. Here, on the primal level of language itself, by which we became the first self-questioning animals, able to assess our own behaviour, is where fiction finds its footing in relation to politics.

My own country, South Africa, provides what can be cited as the paradigm of problems of the full development of the relationship: the wild affair between fiction and politics, with its embraces and repulsions, distress and celebration, loyalty and betrayal. Perhaps echoes of the debate at present in progress over what post-apartheid fiction will be, ought to be, have relevance for the outside world. Of course, the very term 'post-apartheid' fiction reveals the acceptance that there has been such an orthodoxy as 'apartheid' or, more accurately, 'anti-apartheid' fiction. In the long struggle against apartheid, it has been recognized that an oppressed people need the confidence of cultural backing. Literature, fiction including plays and poetry, became what is known as 'a weapon of struggle'. The current debate among us now is between those who, perceiving that the cost was the constraint of the writer's imaginative powers within what was seen narrowly as relevant to the political struggle, think the time has come for writers to release themselves if they are to be imaginatively equal to the fullness of human life predicated for the future, and others who believe literature still must be perceived as a weapon in the hands and under the direction of the liberation movement come to power in a future democracy.

The revolutionary and writer Albie Sachs, with the undeniable authority of one who lost an arm and the sight of one eye in that struggle, has gone so far as to call, if half-seriously (not even the car-bomb was able to damage his lively humour), for a five-year ban on the slogan 'culture is a weapon of struggle'. But, of course, there are some writers who have been—I adapt Seamus Heaney's definition to my own context—'guerrillas of the imagination': in their fiction serving the struggle for freedom by refusing any imposed orthodoxy of subject and treatment, but attempting to take unfettered creative grasp of the complex 'states of things' in which, all through people's lives, directly and indirectly, in dark places and neon light, that struggle has taken place.

Since I am bound to be taken to account about this in relation to my own fiction, I had better answer for myself now. As a citizen, a South African actively opposed to racism all my life, and a supporter and now member of the African National Congress, in my *conduct* and my *actions* I have submitted voluntarily and with self-respect to the discipline of the liberation movement.

For my *fiction* I have claimed and practised my integrity to the free transformation of reality, in whatever forms and modes of expression I need. There, my commitment has been and is to make sense of life as I know it and observe it and experience it. In my ventures into non-fiction, my occasional political essays, my political partisanship has no doubt shown bias, perhaps a selectivity of facts. But then, as I have said before, and stand by: nothing I write in such factual pieces will be as true as my fiction.

So if my fiction and that of other writers has served legitimately the politics I believe in, it has been because the imaginative transformations of fiction, in the words of the Swedish writer Per Wästberg, 'help people understand their own natures and know they are not powerless . . .'

'Every work of art is liberating,' he asserts, speaking for all of us who write. That should be the understanding on which our fiction enters into any relationship with politics, however passionate the involvement may be. The transformation of the imagination must never 'belong' to any establishment, however just, fought-for, and longed-for. Pasternak's words should be our credo:

> *When seats are assigned to passion and vision*
> *on the day of the great assembly*
> *Do not reserve a poet's position:*
> *It is dangerous, if not empty.*

—1988

THE STATUS OF THE WRITER

IN THE WORLD TODAY:

WHICH WORLD? WHOSE WORLD?

A few months ago I was a participant in an international gathering in Paris to evaluate the status of the artist in the world. There we were on an elegant stage before a large audience; among us was a famous musician, a distinguished sculptor, several poets and writers of repute, a renowned dancer-choreographer. We had come together literally from the ends of the earth. At this stately opening session we were flanked by the Director-General of our host organization, the representative of a cultural foundation funded by one of North America's multibillionaire dynasties, and France's Deputy Minister of Culture. The Director-General, the representative of the multibillionaire foundation, and the Deputy Minister each rose and gave an address lasting half an hour; the session, which also was to include some musical performance, was scheduled to close after two hours. An official tiptoed along the backs of our chairs and requested us, the artists, to cut our addresses to three minutes. We humbly took up our pens and began to score out what we had to say. When the bureaucrats had finally regained their seats, we were summoned one by one to speak in telegraphese. All did so except the last in line. She was—I name her in homage!—Mallika Sarabhai, a dancer-choreographer from India. She swept to the podium, a beauty in sandals and sari, and announced: 'I have torn up my speech. The bureaucrats were allowed to speak as long as they pleased; the artists were told that three minutes was time enough for whatever they might have to say. So—we have the answer to the status of the artist in the world today.'

This experience set me thinking back to another that I have had, on a deeper and more personal level.

In my Charles Eliot Norton lectures at Harvard, given in 1994, which subsequently were published under the title *Writing and Being*, I devoted three of the six lectures to the writing and being each of Chinua Achebe, Amos Oz, and Naguib Mahfouz. Edward Said, himself another writer whose work is important to me, reviewed the book extremely favourably in a leading English paper, while yet taking me to task for my indignant assertion that Mahfouz is not given his rightful place in contemporary world literature, is never mentioned in the company of such names as Umberto Eco, Günter Grass, etc., and certainly is not widely read even by those whom one considers well-read; I know that a number of my friends read his work for the first time as a result of my published lecture.

Mahfouz neglected?—Edward Said chided me.

Mahfouz not recognized for his greatness in world literature?

What world did I define him by, what world did my purview confine *me* to in my assessment? In the literature of Arabic culture, the world of the Arabic language, Mahfouz is fully established in the canon of greatness and, in the populist canon of fame, while controversial, is widely read.

Edward Said was right. What I was conceiving of as 'world literature' in my lecture was in fact that of the Euro-North Americans into which only a few of us foreigners have been admitted. Naguib Mahfouz is recognized as a great writer in the world of Arabic literature, of whose canon I know little or nothing.

But wait a moment—Said, I saw, had hit intriguingly upon a paradox. *He* was placing the concept of another 'world literature' alongside the one *I* had posited with my eyes fixed on Euro-North America as the literary navel-of-the-world. In the all-encompassing sense of the term 'world', can any of our literatures be claimed definitively as 'world' literature? Which world? Whose world?

The lesson Edward Said gave me, along with the lesson provided by Mallika Sarabhai at the gathering in Paris, is a sequence, from the situation of artists in general, on the one hand, to the question of literary canons, on the other, that becomes the naturally relevant introduction to my subject, here among my brother and sister African writers: our status, *specifically as writers*, in the worlds-within-'the world' we occupy.

Status. What is status, to us?

First—it never can go without saying—the primary status must be freedom of expression. That is the oxygen of our creativity. Without it, many talents on our continent have struggled for breath; some have choked; and some have been lost to us in that other climate, the thin air of exile.

Suppression of freedom of expression by censorship and bannings was in many of our countries a feature of colonial regimes—I myself was such a victim of the apartheid government, with three of my own works, and an anthology I collected of South African writers' works, banned. Suppression of freedom of expression has continued to be a feature of not a few of our independent regimes, leading outrageously and tragically in one of them, Nigeria, to the execution of one writer and the threat of death sentence placed upon another. But thankfully, in many of our countries, including mine now, South Africa, freedom of expression is entrenched.

Freedom to write. We have that status; and we are fully aware that it is one that we must be always alert to defend against all political rationalisations and pleas to doctor our search for the truth into something more palatable to those who make the compromises of power.

Quite apart from the supreme issue of human freedom, our claim to freedom to write has a significance, a benefit to society that only writers can give. Our books are *necessary*: for in the words of the great nineteenth-century Russian writer Nikolai Gogol they show both the writer and his or her people *what they are*. The writer is both the repository of his people's ethos and his revelation to them of themselves. This revelation is what regimes fear, in their writers. But if our status as writers is to be meaningful, that fear is proof of our integrity . . . And our strength.

Status, like charity, begins at home. The modern movement of African writers to define their status in this century was within our continent itself. With the impact of colonialism and its coefficient industrialisation, the traditional status of the griot, the keeper of the word—which is the generic for one marked for expression of the creative imagination with the 'ring of white chalk round the eye' by Chinua Achebe's old man of Abazon, in *Anthills of the Savannah*—came to an end. It was not, could not be adapted as a status for one whose poetry and stories were disseminated to the people-become-the-public at the remove of printed books, remote from any living presence of their creator in the flesh. The keeper of the word became invisible; had no ready-defined place in society.

I am not going to reiterate the history, including the influence from the African diaspora in the United States and the Caribbean, that both preceded and coincided with the first Congress of Black Writers and Artists in 1956. And it is significant, in terms of progress, to recall that it was not held in Africa at all, but in Paris.

I am looking at the modern movement from the distance made by events between then and now; from the epic unfurling of Africa's freedom from colonial rule in its many avatars, way back from Ghana's, the first, in 1957, to South Africa's, the latest and final one.

In the broad sweep of hindsight one can see that Kwame Nkrumah's political postulation of Pan-Africanism had its cultural equivalent in the movement of négritude. Négritude, as a word, has long become an archaism, with its first syllables— although coming from the French language—suggestive of the American Deep South. But the *other* invented word, with which the young Wole Soyinka cheekily attacked the concept, has remained very much alive because over and over again, in the work of many African writers, Soyinka's iconoclasm has been proved mistaken. 'A tiger doesn't have to proclaim his tigritude', he pronounced. But as each country on our continent has come into its own, in independence, the expression of Africanness, the assertion of African ways of life, from philosophy to food, has intensified: Africa measuring herself against her selfhood, not that of her erstwhile conquerors.

Africanness is fully established. So what status do we writers have, now, right here at home, in our individual countries?

Is it the kind of status we would wish—not in terms of fame and glory, invitations to dine with government ministers, but in terms of the role of literature in the illumination of our people, the opening up of lives to the power and beauty of the imagination, a revelation of themselves by the writer as the repository of a people's ethos? Alongside the establishment of African values—which in the case of our best writers included no fear of questioning some, thus establishing that other essential component of literature's social validity—the criterion in almost all of our countries has been the extent to which the writer has identified with and articulated, through transformations of the creative imagination, the struggle for freedom. And this, then, indeed, was the role of the writer as repository of a people's ethos. Today the status, if to be measured on the scale of political commitment, is more complex.

Yes, economic neo-colonialism is a phase that threatens freedom, in a people's ethos. Yes, the greedy wrangles of the Euro-North American powers to manipulate African political change for the spoils of oil supplies and military influence are concerns in a people's ethos. Yes, the civil wars waged by their own leaders, bringing appalling suffering—these are all part of a people's ethos to be expressed, for now that our continent has rid itself of its self-appointed masters from Europe the sense of identity in having a common enemy has eroded and in many of our countries brotherhood has become that of Cain and Abel.

Between writers and the national state, the threat of death by *fatwa* or secular decree, from Naguib Mahfouz to Ken Saro Wiwa and Wole Soyinka, has become the status of the writer in some of our countries. Yet these and less grim political themes tend to be the mise-en-scène of contemporary writing on our continent rather than its centrality. Africanism itself is an economic and cultural concept rather than an ideological one, now. For writers, the drama of individual and personal relations that was largely suppressed in themselves, and when indulged in was judged by their societies as trivial in comparison with the great shared traumas of the liberation struggle, now surfaces. There is so much to write about that was pushed aside by the committed creative mind, before; and there is so much to write about that never happened, couldn't exist, before. Freedom and its joys, and—to paraphrase Freud—freedom and its discontents, are the ethos of a people for its writers now.

So we have lost the status of what one might call national engagement we had. Some few of us take on the responsibility to become writer-politicians and diplomats. But there are unlikely to be any future Léopold Sédar Senghors, poet-presidents. And I ask myself, and you: Do we writers seek, need that nature of status, the writer as politician, states-person? Is it not thrust upon us, as a patriotic duty outside the particular gifts we have to offer? Is not the ring of chalk round the eye the sign of our true calling? Whatever else we are called upon to do takes us away from the dedication we know our role as writers requires of us. As the cultural arm of liberation struggles, we met the demands of our time in that era. That was our national status. We have yet to be recognized with a status commensurate with respect for the primacy of the well-earned role of *writer-as-writer* in the post-colonial era.

How would we ourselves define such a status?

What do we expect, of our governments, our societies, and—in return—expect to give of ourselves to these? I have personally decisive convictions about this, constantly evolving as the country I belong to develops its cultural directions, and I am sure you have your convictions, ideas. And we need to exchange them, East–West, North–South, across our continent—that, indeed, is my first conviction. We need to meet in the flesh, take one another's hands, hear one another.

But you and I know that the best there is in us, as writers, is in our books. The benefit and pleasure of personal contact is, in any case, limited to a fortunate few. Much more important, we need to read one another's work. We and the people of our countries need natural and easy access to the writings that express the ethos of our neighbouring countries: what they believe, what they feel, how they make their way through the hazards and joys of living, contained by what varieties of socio-political and cultural structures they are in the process of pursuing. Four decades after the first country to attain independence, in the libraries and bookshops of our countries you still will find, apart from works by the writers of each country itself, only a handful of books by the same well-known names among African writers from other countries of our continent. Every now and then, there may be a new one, a Ben Okri who comes to us by way of recognition in Europe, along the old North–South cultural conduit. Without the pioneering work of Hans Zell, and the invaluable Heinemann African Writers Series, the publication of journals, from the old *Présence Africaine* to those bravely launched, often to a short or uneven life, by writers' organizations or publishers in our various countries, the cross-pollination of literature in Africa would scarcely exist where it should: among ordinary readers rather than the African literati we represent, here. The best part of two generations has gone by since the African continent began its inexorable achievement of independence that has now culminated: a priority in our claim for the status of writers and writing in Africa surely is that there should be developed a Pan-African network of publishers and distributors who will co-operate—greatly to their own commercial advantage, by the way—to make our writers' work as prominently and naturally available as the Euro-North American potboilers which fill airport bookstalls. This does not mean that we should export potboilers to one another! It means that writing of quality which readers in your countries and mine never see, unless they happen to have the resources to come across and mail-order from specialist book catalogues, would be beside our beds at night and in our hands as we travel on buses, trains, and planes.

You will say that the old obstacle of our Babel's Tower of languages rises before an African network of publishing. But the fact is that colonial conquest, with all its destruction and deprivation, ironically left our continent with a short list of *lingue franche* that have been appropriated to Africa's own ends in more ways than pragmatic communication for politics and trade. English, French, and Portuguese—these three at least are the languages used by many African writers in their work—for good or ill in relation to national culture: that is another whole debate that will continue. These three languages have virtually become *adjunct African languages by rightful appropriation*; and the translation into them of African language literature, which itself is and always must be the foundation and ultimate criterion of the continent's literature, is not an obstacle but an opportunity. Where are the translation centres at our colleges and universities, where young scholars could gain deep insights into their own languages while learning the skills of translation? Here is a field of cultural advancement, cultural employment in *collaboration with publishers*, waiting to be cultivated. We have an OAU uniting our continent, sometimes in contention as well as common purpose, on matters of mutual concern in international affairs, governance, policy, and trade; we need an OAC, an Organization of African Culture, to do the same for Pan-African literature and the arts. Only then should we have a 'world literature': the world of our own, our challenge to the title each culturo-political and linguistic grouping on our planet has the hubris to claim for itself.

Professor Lebona Mosia, an arts academic in South Africa, recently reflected on our Deputy President Thabo Mbeki's concept of an African renaissance of roots, values, and identity, remarking that our people are emerging from an 'imaginary history . . . whose white folks believed that South Africa is part of Europe, America (the USA) and Australia. Blacks have always recognized that they are part of Africa'. The same 'imaginary history' of course applies to Pan Africa, to the thinking of all ex-colonial powers.

Does Thabo Mbeki's renaissance sound like a renaissance of négritude?

I don't believe it is. Or could be. Circumstances in our countries have changed so fundamentally since that concept of the 1950s, when liberation was still to be won. The reality of African history has long begun to be recorded and established, from where it was cut off as anthropology and prehistory and substituted by the history of foreign conquest and settlers. One of the dictionary definitions of the wide meanings of renaissance is 'any revival in art and literature'; as we writers take to ourselves the right to vary or add to the meaning of words, I would interpret the meaning of renaissance in Mbeki's context not as reviving the past, whether pre-colonial or of the négritude era, but of using it only as a basis for cultural self-realisation and development in an Africa that *never existed before*, because it is an Africa that has *come through*: emerged from the experience of slavery, colonial oppression, the humiliating exploitation of paternalism, economic and spiritual degradation, suffering of every nature human evil could devise. A continent that has liberated itself; overcome.

Africans have established, beyond question, that our continent is not part of anyone's erstwhile empire. Secure in this confidence, and open-eyed at home as I hope we shall be to the necessity to apply ourselves to developing Africa's literary variety to-and-fro across our own Pan-African frontiers, it's time to cross new frontiers on our cultural horizon, to turn the literary compass to measure whether we still should be pointing in the same direction towards the outside world.

Which world? Whose world? The North–South axis was the one on which we were regarded so long only as on the receiving end, and which, latterly, we have somewhat culturally reversed: African writers have won prestigious literary prizes in England and France, and even Nobel Prizes; African music has become popular abroad, the international fashion industry presently has a vogue for somewhat bizarre adaptations of African traditional dress—well, Africa dressed itself up in Europe's three-piece suits, collar, and tie; now *haute couture* Europe wraps itself in a *pagne*, a dashiki, a bou-bou . . .

Of course we do, and should, retain our freedom of access to, appropriation of, European and North American literary culture. I believe we have passed the stage, in the majority of our countries, of finding Shakespeare and Dostoevsky, Voltaire and Melville, 'irrelevant'. I believe that, as writers and readers, all literature of whatever origin *belongs* to us. There *is* an acceptable 'world literature' in this sense; one great library to which it would be a folly of self-deprivation to throw away our membership cards.

What *has* happened is that the works of our own writers, imparting the ethos of our peoples, have firmly and rightfully displaced those of Europeans as the definitive cultural texts in our schools and universities.

But if you place the compass on a map you will see not alone that South–South and not North–South is our closer orientation, but that if you cut out the shape of South America and that of Africa you can fit the east coast of South America and the west coast of Africa together, pieces of a jigsaw puzzle making a whole—the lost continent Gondwana, sundered by cosmic cataclysms and seas.

This romantic geographical connection is merely symbolic of the actual, potential relationships that lay dormant and ignored during the colonial period when our continent of Africa was set by European powers strictly on the North–South axis. Climate and terrain are primary experiences for human beings; many South American and African countries share the same kind of basic natural environment, which determines not only the types of food they grow and eat, but the myths they created, and the nature of city life they have evolved. Both continents were conquered by European powers, their culture over-run and denigrated. Both have won their freedom from foreign powers through suffering, and suffered subsequently under brutal dictators in internecine wars among their own people. Both bear a burden of their people's poverty and confront neo-colonialism exacted in return for their need of economic aid. Finally, there is the strange reciprocal bond: with those communities in South America descended from slaves brought from Africa.

All this in common, and yet we know so little of South American writers' work and life. Aside from some few big names, such as Borges of Argentina, Machado de Assis of Brazil, Mario Vargas Llosa of Peru, Octavio Paz and Carlos Fuentes of Mexico, Gabriel García Márquez of Colombia, we do not know the work of the majority of South American writers, with whom, in many ways, we have more *existential* ties than with writers in Europe and North America.

Industrialists and entrepreneurs are opening up their South–South routes of trade, matching the exchange of raw materials, processing, and expertise which countries in South America and Africa can supply for one another. They are giving more than a side-glance away from the fixed gaze of North–South development. Recently the poet Mongane Wally Serote and I visited Argentina, Brazil, and Uruguay, and there met writers from other South American countries, as well. All were eager to grow closer to their recognition that our literatures are reciprocal in the ethos of our many shared existential situations, from the colonised past to the development problems of the present, both material and cultural. If the industrialists and entrepreneurs are paying attention to the material reciprocity, why are we, as writers, not looking South–South in a new freedom to choose which world, whose world, beyond our own with which we could create a wider one for ourselves?

In our first concern, which is to develop an African 'world literature' as our status, we should keep well in mind the words of the great Mexican poet Octavio Paz. With the exceptions of the pre-Hispanic civilisations of America, he writes, all civilisations—including China and Japan—have been the result of intersections and clashes with foreign cultures. And the Congolais writer Henri Lopès, in his novel *Le Lys et le Flamboyant*, is speaking not only of the mixed blood of tribe, race, and colour of many of our people in Africa, but of the interchange of ideas, of solutions to a common existence, when he writes, 'Every civilisation is born of a forgotten mixture, every race is a variety of mixtures that is ignored.' The nurture of our writers, our literature, is a priority which should not create for us a closed-shop African 'world literature', a cultural exclusivity in place of the exclusion, even post-colonial, that has kept us in an ante-room of self-styled 'world literatures'. Let our chosen status in the world be that of writers who seek exchanges of the creative imagination, ways of thinking and writing, of fulfilling the role of repository of the people's ethos, by opening it out, bringing to it a vital mixture of individuals and peoples re-creating themselves.

Finally, at home in Africa, in the countries of our continent, let Rosa Luxemburg's definition be at the tip of our ballpoint pens and on the screens of our word-processors as we write: 'Freedom means freedom to those who think differently.' Let the writer's status be recognized as both praise singer and social critic. Let's say with Amu Djoleto:

> *What you expect me to sing, I will not,*
> *What you do not expect me to croak, I will.*

—2nd PAWA Annual Lecture, Pan African Writers Association
5th International African Writers' Day Celebration
Accra, Ghana, 1–7 November 1997

TURNING THE PAGE:

AFRICAN WRITERS AND

THE TWENTY-FIRST CENTURY

W riters in Africa in the twentieth century, now coming to an end, have interpreted the greatest events on our continent since the abolition of slavery.

We have known that our task was to bring to our people's consciousness and that of the world the true dimensions of racism and colonialism beyond those that can be reached by the newspaper column and screen image, however valuable these may be. We have sought the fingerprint of flesh on history.

The odds against developing as a writer able to take on this huge responsibility have been great for most of our writers. But as Agostinho Neto, Angolan poet and president, said, and proved in his own life: 'If writing is one of the conditions of your being alive, you create that condition.'

Out of adversity, out of oppression, in spite of everything . . .

Looking forward into the twenty-first century, I think we have the right to assess what we have come through. Being here; the particular time and place that has been twentieth-century Africa. This has been a position with particular implications for literature; we have lived and worked through fearful epochs. Inevitably, the characteristic of African literature during the struggle against colonialism and, latterly, neo-colonialism and corruption in post-colonial societies, has been engagement—political engagement.

Now, unfortunately, many people see this concept of engagement as a limited category closed to the range of life reflected in literature; it is regarded as some sort of upmarket version of propaganda. Engagement is not understood for what it really has been, in the hands of honest and talented writers: the writer's exploration of the particular meaning his or her being has taken on in this time and place. For real 'engagement', for the writer, isn't something set apart from the range of the creative imagination. It isn't something dictated by brothers and sisters in the cause he or she shares with them. It comes from within the writer, his or her creative destiny, living in history. 'Engagement' doesn't preclude the beauty of language, the complexity of human emotions; on the contrary, such literature must be able to use all these in order to be truly engaged with life, where the overwhelming factor in that life is political struggle.

While living and writing under these conditions in Africa, we have seen our books banned—and we have gone on writing. Many of our writers, including Wole Soyinka, have been imprisoned, and many, including Chinua Achebe, Dennis Brutus, Nuruddin Farah, have been forced to choose exile. I think of immensely talented Can Themba, Alex La Guma, and Dambudzo Marechera, who died there; lost to us.

.   .   .

What do we in Africa hope to achieve, as writers, in the new century? Because we are writers, can we expect to realize literally, through our work, that symbol of change, the turning to a fresh page?

What are the conditions under which we may expect to write—ideological, material, social?

It seems to me that these are the two basic questions for the future of African literature. I think it's generally agreed that consonance with the needs of the people is the imperative for the future in our view of our literature. This is the point of departure from the past; there, literature played the immeasurably valuable part of articulating the people's political struggle, but I do not believe it can be said to have enriched their lives with a literary culture. And I take it that our premise, in Africa, is that a literary culture is a people's right.

We all make the approach from our experience in the twentieth century. We all hazard predictions, since we do not know in what circumstances our ambitions for a developing literature will need to be carried out. We have our ideas and convictions of how literary development should be consonant with the needs of our people; we cannot know with what manner of political and social orders we shall have to seek that consonance.

I think we have to be completely open-eyed about the relation between our two basic questions. We have to recognize that the first—what we hope to achieve in terms of literary directions—is heavily dependent on the second: the conditions under which we shall be working as writers. A literary culture cannot be created by writers without readers. There are no readers without adequate education. It's as simple—and dire—as that. No matter how much we encourage writers who are able to fulfill, according to their talents, the various kinds and levels of writing that will take literature out of the forbidding context of unattainable intellectualism, we shall never succeed until there is a wide readership competent beyond school-primer and comic-book level. And where there are readers there must be libraries where the new literature we hope to nurture, satisfying the need of identification with people's own daily lives, and the general literature that brings the great mind-opening works of the world to them, are easily available to them.

Will these potential readers find prose, poetry, and non-fiction in their mother tongues?

If we are to create a twenty-first-century African literature, how is this to be done while publishing in African languages remains mainly confined to works prescribed for study, market-stall booklets, religious tracts? We have long accepted that Africa cannot, and so far as her people are concerned, has no desire to, create a 'pure' culture in linguistic terms; this is an anachronism when for purposes of material development the continent eagerly seeks means of technological development from all over the world.

We all know that there is no such workable system as a purely indigenous economy once everyone wants computers and movie cassettes.

Neither, in a future of increasing intercontinental contact, can there be a 'pure' indigenous culture. We see, a plain fact all over Africa, that the European languages that came with colonial conquest have been taken over into independence, *acquired* by Africans and made part and parcel of their own convenience and culture. The brilliant examples of this acquisition are there to be read in the work of some black African writers. (Whites, of course, have never had the good sense to do the same with African languages . . .)

But we writers cannot speak of taking up the challenge of a new century for African literature unless writing in African languages becomes the major component of the continent's literature. Without this, one cannot speak of an African literature. It must be the basis of the cultural cross-currents that will both buffet and stimulate that literature.

What of publishing?

We write the books; to come alive, they have to be read. To be available, they have to be competently distributed, not only in terms of libraries, but also commercially. Many of us in Africa have had experience of trying to meet the needs of the culturally marginalised by launching small, non-profit publishing ventures in African literature. We find ourselves stopped short by the fact that the distribution network, certainly in the southern African countries (I don't imagine there is much difference in countries to the north), remains the same old colonial one. Less than a handful of distribution networks make decisions, based on the lowest common denominator of literary value, on what books should be bought from publishers, and this handful has the only means of distributing these widely to the public, since they own the chain bookstores which dominate the trade in the cities and are the only existing bookstores in most small towns. In South Africa, for example, in the twentieth century, there have been and are virtually *no* bookstores in the vast areas where blacks have been confined under apartheid.

Another vital question: What will be the various African states' official attitude to culture, and to literature as an expression of that culture? We writers don't know, and have every reason to be uneasy. Certainly, in the twentieth century of political struggle, state money has gone into guns, not books; literature, culture, has been relegated to the dispensable category. As for literacy, so long as people can read state decrees and the graffiti that defy them, that has been regarded as sufficient proficiency. As writers, do we envisage, for example, a dispensation from a Ministry of Culture in South Africa to fund publishing in African languages, and to provide libraries in rural communities and in the shanty towns which no doubt will be with us, still, for a long time? Would we have to fear that, in return for subvention, writers might be restricted by censorship of one kind or another? How can we ensure that our implicit role—supplying a critique of society for the greater understanding and enrichment of life there—will be respected?

Considering all these factors that stand against the writer's act of transforming literature in response to a new era, it seems that we writers have, however reluctantly, to take on contingent responsibilities that should not be ours. We'll have to concern ourselves with the quality and direction of education—will our schools turn out drones or thinkers? How shall we press for a new policy and structure of publishing and distribution, so that writers may write in African languages and bring pleasure and fulfillment to thousands who are cut off from literature by lack of knowledge of European languages? How shall we make the function of writers, whose hand held out to contribute to development is in the books they offer, something recognized and given its value by the governing powers of the twenty-first century? We have to begin now to concern ourselves with the structures of society that contain culture, and within which it must assert its growth.

And there is yet one more problem to be faced by the naked power of the word, which is all we have, but which has proved itself unkillable by even the most horrible of conventional and unconventional weaponry. Looking back, many well-known factors inhibited the growth of a modern African culture, an African literature, in the century whose sands are running out through our fingers. One hardly need cite the contemptuous dismissal of all African culture by frontier and colonial domination; the cementing-over of African music, dance, myth, philosophy, religious beliefs, and secular rituals: the very stuff on which the literary imagination feeds. The creativity of Africa lay ignored beneath the treading feet of white people on their way to see the latest Hollywood gangster movie or to pick up from the corner store a comic with bubble text in American. And soon, soon, these were joined by black people in the same pursuit, having been convinced, since everything that was their own was said to be worthless, that this was the culture to acquire. The habit of chewing cultural pulp is by now deeply established among our people. And it is so temptingly cheap to be bought from abroad by our media, including the dominant cultural medium of our time, television, that literature in Africa not only has to express the lives of the people but also has to assert the beauty and interest of this reality against mega-subculture—the new opium of the people . . .

Surely the powers of the imagination of our writers can be exerted to attract our people away from the soporific sitcom, surely the great adventures that writers explore in life can offer a child something as exciting in image and word as the cumbersome battle between Japanese turtles? We in Africa don't want cultural freedom hijacked by the rush of international sub-literature into the space for growth hard-won by ourselves in the defeat of colonial culture. That is perhaps the greatest hazard facing us as we turn the page of African literature and write the heading: twenty-first century.

—UNESCO Symposium
Harare, Zimbabwe, 1992

REFERENCES:

THE CODES OF CULTURE

———⟶●⟵———

When I am asked that interviewer's stock-in-trade, 'For whom do you write?', I reply irritatedly, 'For anyone who reads me.'

The question is crass, giving away the media's assumption that a writer, like itself, presumes 'readership potential'. It seems typical of the anti-art tenet of commercialism: give the public what they know. But writers—artists of all kinds—exist to break up the paving of habit and breach the railings that confine sensibility; free imaginative response to spring up like grass. We are convinced that we are able to release the vital commonality of the human psyche, our reach limited only by the measure of our talent. After all, isn't this what we ourselves have received at the touch of other writers? If we are not manufacturing for Mills and Boon, if we are not writing political tracts disguised as works of the imagination, we do not have in mind a shadow company of heads out there, the chat-show groupies or the Party supporters.

But for some time, now, I have felt a certain unease when I snap, 'Anyone who reads me.' The echo comes: 'Oh really? My, my!' I begin to think there *is* a question to be asked, but it is not 'For whom do we write?' It is 'For whom *can* we write?' Is there not such a thing as writer potential, perhaps? The postulate reversed? And may I dismiss that one high-handedly? These doubts—or more accurately suggestions—have come about in my particular case less from readings in literary theory over the years than as a result of experience out there in the world among—not ordinary people, to a writer no-one is ordinary—among non-literary people. Which does not imply that they do not read, only that their reading does not take place in the matrix of culture most literature presupposes.

And here there must be a self-correction again. The suggestions are raised as much by the contradictions between literary theory—which, of course, is concerned with the reader's perceptions as well as the writer's conscious and subconscious intentions—and the actual life experience of the man or woman on the receiving end of all these deliberations: the generic reader. For the generic reader surely must be the one I have in mind when I answer that I write for 'anyone who reads me'?

More than twenty years ago, we were all entranced by or sceptical of (or both at once) the discoveries of structuralism and its analysis of our art and our relationship to the reader. The Freudian explanations we had gone by seemed simplistic and speculative by comparison. The subconscious was ectoplasm in contrast with the precise methodology of a work such as, say, Roland Barthes' *S/Z*, published in 1970 on the basis of work done in the sixties. The whole emphasis of literature passed from writer to reader. Barthes' goal was 'to make the reader no longer a consumer but a producer of the text', of 'what can be read but not written'. The novel, the short story, the poem, were redefined as a 'galaxy of signifiers'. As Richard Howard sums up, Barthes' conviction of reading was: 'What is told is always the telling'. And Harry Levin wrote: 'To survey his [the writer's] writings in their totality and chart the contours of their "inner Landscape" is the critical aim of current Structuralists and Phenomenologists. All of these approaches recognize, as a general principle, that every writer has his own configuration of ideas and sentiments, capacities and devices.'

Barthes' brilliance, with its element of divine playfulness, made and makes enthralling reading—for those of us who share at least sufficient of his cultural matrix to gain aesthetic pleasure and revelation from his cited 'signifiers'. It's a detective game, in which the satisfaction comes from correctly interpreting the clue—elementary, for Sherlock Holmes, but not for my dear Watson. Barthes, in the structural analysis of Balzac's novella *Sarrasine*, is the Sherlock Holmes who, deducing from his immensely rich cultural experience, instantly recognizes the fingerprints of one cultural reference upon another. The reader is Watson, for whom, it may be, the 'signifier' signifies nothing but itself, if there is nothing in the range of his cultural experience for it to be referred *to*. It is a swatch that does not match any colour in his spectrum, a note that cannot be orchestrated in his ear. So that even if he is told that Balzac's clock of the Elysée Bourbon is actually chiming metonymic reference to the Faubourg Saint-Honoré, and from the Faubourg Saint-Honoré to the Paris of the Bourbon Restoration, and then to the Restoration as a 'mythic place of sudden fortunes whose origins are suspect'—there remains a blank where that reader is supposed to be reading 'what is not written'. The signifier works within a closed system: it presupposes a cultural context shared by writer and reader beyond literacy. Without that resource the reader cannot 'read' the text in Barthean abundance. 'Words are symbols that assume a shared memory', says Borges. The

Faubourg Saint-Honoré is just the name of a district, it has no elegant social/intellectual associations, either as an image conjured up from visits to Paris or as a symbol described in other books, visualized in paintings. The Bourbon Restoration brings no association as a 'mythic place of sudden fortunes whose origins are suspect' because the reader doesn't know the place of the Bourbon Restoration in French political and social history. The polymath interchange of the arts, letters, politics, history, philosophy, taken for granted by Barthes, is not the traffic of that reader's existence.

When one says one writes for 'anyone who reads me' one must be aware that 'anyone' excludes a vast number of readers who cannot 'read' you or me because of givens they do not share with us in unequal societies. The Baudelairean correspondences of earlier literary theory cannot work for them, either, because 'correspondence' implies the recognition of one thing in terms of another, which can occur only *within the same cultural resource system.*

This is the case even for those of us, like me, who believe that books are not made out of other books, but out of life. Whether we like it or not, we can be 'read' only by readers who share terms of reference formed in us by our education— not merely academic but in the broadest sense of life experience; our political, economic, social, and emotional concepts, and our values derived from these; our cultural matrix. It remains true even of those who have put great distances between themselves and the inducted values of childhood; who have changed countries, convictions, ways of life, languages. Citizenship of the world is merely another acculturation, with its set of givens that may derive from many cultures yet in combination becomes something that is not any of them.

Posing to himself the big question, 'For whom do we write?', Italo Calvino wrote: 'Given the division of the world into a capitalist camp, an imperialist camp and a revolutionary camp, whom is the writer writing for?'

While—if he has any sense—refusing to write for any camp, despite personal political loyalties (and I think there are more of them than Calvino allows), the writer certainly writes from *within* one of them. And the reader reads from *within* one. If it is not the same as that of the writer, he is presumed at least to 'read' in the writer's signifiers some relevance to his own, different cultural matrix. But frequently the reader does not find equivalents, in that culture, for the writer's referential range, because he has not 'read' that range. He cannot. The signifying image, word, flashes a message that cannot be received by a different set of preconceptions. This happens even at apparently homogenous cultural levels. In reviews of your fiction and the interviews to which you are subjected, this process can hatch in your text like a cuckoo's egg. What comes out is unrecognizable, but the reader, the reviewer, journalist, insists that it is yours.

I experienced this when I came to the United States for the publication of a novel of mine entitled *Burger's Daughter*. The daughter and other characters in the story were centred round the personality of Lionel Burger, exemplifying the phenomenon—and problem—of ideology as faith in the family of an Afrikaner who, through becoming a Communist, devotes his life and theirs to the liberation of South Africa from apartheid. In reviews, Burger was unfailingly referred to as a liberal; I myself perpetrated the unthinkable lack of deference to a famous talk-show personality when I contradicted his description of Burger as a noble white liberal.

He's not a liberal, he's a Communist, I interrupted.

But it was no good. None of these people 'read' me because in the ethos of mainstream American society a Communist could never be, no matter in what country or social circumstances, a good man. Yet it had to be acknowledged that Burger was a good man because he was a fighter against racism; therefore my signal must be that Burger was a liberal. This is not a matter of misreading or misunderstanding. It is the substitution of one set of values for another, *because the reader cannot conceive of these otherwise.*

Yet not politics but class most calls into question the existence of the generic reader, the 'whoever reads me'. And by class I mean to signify economics, education, and, above all, living conditions. The cultural context from laws to latrines, from penthouse to poorhouse, travelled by jet or on foot.

I grant that the difference between the material conditions of life signified in the text and those of the reader must be extreme, and manifest in the dogged daily experience of the reader, if the writer cannot be 'read' by him. As the seventeen-year-old daughter of a shopkeeper in a small mining town in Africa, I was able to 'read' *The Remembrance of Things Past*. Why? Because, although the lineage Proust invented, so faithful to that of the French noblesse, genuine and parvenue, could not signify for me, the familial mores from which the novel sets out, so to speak, and are there throughout—the way emotions are expressed in behaviour between mother and child, the place of friendship in social relations, the exaltation of sexuality as romantic love, the regulation of daily life by meals and visits, the importance of maladies—all this was within the context of middle-class experience, however far-flung.

And by the way, from where did I get the book? Why, the municipal library; and I could use the library because I was white—and so for me that also was part of the middle-class

experience. No black could use that library; in the concommi-
tance of class and colour a young black person of my age was
thus doubly excluded from 'reading' Proust's Méséglise and the
Guermantes Ways: by lack of any community of cultural background, and by racist material conditions . . .

Hermeneutic differences between writer and reader are still
extreme in our world, despite the advance in technological
communications. There is a layer of common culture spread
thin over the worlds, first, second, and third, by satellite and
cassette. The writer could count on the 'signifier' 'Dallas' or
'Rambo' to be received correctly and fully by any reader from
Iceland to Zimbabwe, and almost any other points on the map
culturally remote from one another. But the breadth of this
potential readership paradoxically limits the writer; producing,
it would seem, something close to the generic reader, it confines
the writer to a sort of primer of culture, if he expects truly to be
'read'. It excludes signifiers that cannot be spelt out in that
ABC. The writer's expectations of readership have diminished
in inverse proportion to the expansion of technological communications.

And the effect of extreme differences in material conditions
between writer and reader remains decisive. Such differences
affect profoundly the imagery, the relativity of values, the referential interpretation of events between the cultural givens of
most writers and, for example, the new class of industrial workers, emancipated by the surplus value of leisure earned first by
mechanisation and then computerisation. Writers, longing to
be 'read' by anyone who reads them, from time to time attempt
to overcome this in various and curious ways. John Berger has
experimented by going to live among peasants, trying to enter
into their life-view as formed by their experience. He writes
about their lives in a mode that signifies for us, who are not

French peasants; we 'read' him with all our experience we share with him of literary exoticism, of life-as-literature providing the necessary layers of references. He doesn't say whether the peasants read what he writes; but remarks that they are aware that he has access to something they don't have, 'another body of knowledge, a knowledge of the surrounding but distant world'. A recent review of one of Bobbie Ann Mason's books sums up the general problem: 'She writes the kind of fiction her characters would never read.'

In South Africa there has been demonstrated recently an ostensibly wider potential readership for writers within our population of 29 million, only five million of whom are white. Politically motivated, in the recognition that the encouragement of literature is part of liberation, trade unions and community groups among the black population have set up makeshift libraries and cultural debate. Now, I do not believe that one should ever underestimate the powers of comprehension of anyone who is literate. I don't believe anyone should be written down to. (Had I been confined in this way I certainly never would have become a writer.) Once the love of literature ignites, it can consume many obstacles to understanding. The vocabulary grows in proportion to the skills of the writer in providing imaginative leaps. But these must *land* somewhere recognizable; and most writers share no givens with the kind of potential readership I have just described.

In Africa and many places elsewhere, John Updike's beautifully-written genre stories of preoccupation with divorces and adulteries could touch off no referential responses in readers for whom sexual and family life are determined by circumstances of law and conflict that have no referents in the professional class of suburban North America. The domestic traumas of black South Africans are children imprisoned in detention, lovers fleeing the country from security police, plastic shelters demolished by the authorities and patched together again by husband and wife. The novels of Gabriel García Márquez, himself a socialist, presuppose an answering delight in the larger-than-life that can find little response in those whose own real experience outdoes all extremes, the solitudes of apartheid surpassing any hundred years of solitude. The marvellous fantasies of an Italo Calvino require givens between writer and reader that are not merely a matter of sophistication.

Life is not like that for this readership. Books are not (Barthes) made of other books, for them. Furthermore, the imaginative projection of what life *might be like* is not like that. These texts cannot be 'read' even in terms of aspirations. Surely this is true of serious writers in and from most countries where material conditions do not remotely correspond with those of the reader.

It is most obvious in South Africa. White writers, living as part of an over-privileged minority, are worlds away from those of a migratory miner living in a single-sex hostel, a black schoolteacher grappling with pupils who risk their lives as revolutionaries, black journalists, doctors, clerks, harassed by the police and vigilantes round their homes. The gap sometimes seems too great to reach across for even the most talented and sensitive power of empathy and imaginative projection. I am not saying, nor do I believe, that whites cannot write about blacks, or blacks about whites. Even black writers, who share with these readers disaffection and humiliation under racist laws, generally acquire middle-class or privileged unconventional styles of living and working concommitant with middle-class signifiers, as they make their way as writers. Often it is only by a self-conscious effort of memory—using the signifiers of childhood, before they joined the elite of letters, or drawing on the collective memory of an oral tradition—that they can be sure they will be 'read' by these readers. Freedom of movement—week-end trips, stays in hotels, choice of occupation—which punctuates the lives of many fictional characters, signifies nothing to the migratory worker whose contract does not allow him to stay on in town if he changes jobs, and whose 'holiday' at the end of eighteen months down a mine is the return home to plough and sow. The cosseted white adolescent who rebels against the materialism of parents signifies nothing to the child revolutionaries, often precociously intelligent, an increasing phenomenon in Latin America as well as South Africa, who have abandoned parents, never known home comforts, and taken on life-and-death decisions for themselves. Even among white-collar readers of this milieu, existential anguish—Sartre's nausea or Freud's discontents—finds no answering association where there is a total preoccupation with the business of survival. *The Spoils of Poynton* cannot be read as the apotheosis of the cult of possession by someone who has never seen such objects to covet, someone whose needs would not correspond to any attraction they are presupposed to have— that 'given' attraction taken as read, by the writer.

You might well object: Who expects a poorly-educated clerk or teacher to read Henry James? But, as I have tried to illustrate, many signifiers that are commonplace, assumed, in the cultural code of the writer find no referents in that of the potential wider readership.

What can the writer count on if she/he obstinately persists that one can write for anyone who picks up one's book? Even the basic emotions, love, hate, fear, joy, sorrow, often find expression in a manner that has no correspondence between one code of culture and another. The writer may count on the mythic, perhaps. On a personification of fears, for example, recognizable and surviving from the common past of the subconscious, when we were all in the cave together, there were as yet no races, no classes, and our hairiness hid differences in colour. The prince who has turned into a frog and the beetle Gregory who wakes up to find himself transformed into are avatars of the fear of being changed into something monstrous, whether by the evil magic of a shaman or by psychological loss of self, that signify across all barriers, including that of time. They can be 'read' by anyone, everyone. But how few of us, the writers, can hope ever to create the crystal ball in which meaning can be read, pure and absolute; it is the vessel of genius, which alone, now and then, attains universality in art.

For the rest of us, there is no meta-culture. We ought to be modest in our claims. There is no generic reader, out there.

The kiss of the millennium when art shall be universal understanding shows no sign of being about to release us from our limitations.

—1989

THE LION, THE BULL,

AND THE TREE

—————◄►————

Léopold Sédar Senghor's life almost spans the twentieth century; but he is a man of the century in a way more important than longevity. He embodies the entire black experience, for slavery was still in the living memory of old Africans when he was born, and by the time of his ninetieth birthday the freedom cry from South Africa, *mayibuye*—Come back, Africa, return from colonisation to possess your African self—had been realized over the whole continent, including the final arsenal of white racist rule, South Africa itself.

Africa has many heroes to name, but surely none has quite the relevance to the present, in synergistic terms, that Senghor has. He made of himself a great poet and a powerful political leader; a feat that would seem impossible, for the pragmatic compromises that presidential leadership demands invariably sacrifice and plummet to earth, wounded, the creative imagination of the poet. (Look at the silence that has fallen upon the poet in Presi-

dent Václav Hável.) Senghor created, with Aimé Césaire, the
separatist movement of négritude, drawing from the then youthful Wole Soyinka the cheeky riposte, 'A tiger doesn't have to
proclaim his tigritude.' Senghor became a distinguished scholar,
extolling the language of the coloniser, lecturing on their own
literature to the conquerors of his own country, the French. He
was a Deputy in France's Assemblée Nationale, and an African
socialist in the movement of liberation for his country from
French rule; he is a devout Catholic and a brilliantly eloquent
expositor of traditional African beliefs and philosophy, the
power of the African ethos versus Christianity.

He has made of these apparent irreconcilables a new man;
the new African, a prototype that most of the rest of the continent hasn't caught up with yet.

It is fascinating to follow this extraordinary adventure of the
human spirit. Senghor has never spared himself exploration of
the fundaments which underlie human divergences; secondary
causes were not the easy choices he would take: the established
categories of racism—prejudice explained by white primitivism, reaction to black skin. For me, his most profound piece
of philosophical thinking is 'The African Apprehension of Reality', which is also a daring foray into its concommitant, the
white apprehension of reality. For apprehension is no less than
the first principle of consciousness, the beginning of everything,
our place in relation to nature and our perceptions of fellow
human beings. Ironically—perhaps because that was the moral
hierarchy established by the colonial milieu into which he was
born—he commences with the white apprehension, as a measure set up. 'Let us consider first the European as he faces an
object . . . He first distinguishes the object from himself. He
keeps it at a distance. He freezes it out of time and, in a way,
out of space . . . He makes a *means* of it. He destroys it by

devouring it. "White men are cannibals", an old sage in my own country told me . . . "It is this process of devouring which they call humanizing nature or more exactly domesticating nature . . . they don't take into account that life cannot be domesticated." '

To this Senghor opposes: 'The African is as it were shut up inside his black skin. He lives in primordial night. He does not begin by distinguishing himself from the object, the tree or stone, the man or animal or social event. He does not keep it at a distance. He does not analyse it . . . He turns it over and over in his supple hands, he fingers it, he *feels* it. The African is . . . a pure sensory field. Subjectively, at the end of his antennae, like an insect, he discovers the *Other*.'

These existential dicta could and do rouse hackles of accusation: the apprehension attributed to the whites is racist and derogatory, and that attributed to the blacks is obeisance to a romantic primitivism that so easily can be used by whites to 'prove' that blacks are childish and backward. Of course, Senghor's thesis is that in order to free him or herself from alienation, the human must not lose in the isolation of cerebration his/her invaluable sensuous connections with all creation. As for the charge of slavish romanticising of black sensibilities, the existential state he claims for these is strikingly similar to the concept of living in tune with universal energy extolled in a great philosophy-cum-way-of-life, at the other side of the world, the Vedanta.

Senghor goes beyond what most analysts of the human condition do in identifying the divisions separating one form of apprehension of existence from another. He not only posits a dilemma, asks a question; he proceeds to solve it in himself, to provide an answer. Sometimes in surprisingly curious ways, unafraid, as always, of inevitable criticism from his own people—the hardest

to bear. Having characterised Europeans as 'white cannibals' who
devour life instead of celebrating their place and shared purpose
in it with all living things, he asks, in a poem dedicated to a president of France, no less than Georges Pompidou:

> *Lord God, forgive white Europe.*
> *It is true, Lord, that for four enlightened centuries, she has*
> *scattered the baying and slaver of her mastiffs over my land*
> *and opened my heavy eyelids to the light of faith;*
> *who opened my heart to the understanding of the world,*
> *showing me the rainbow of fresh faces that are my brothers'.*

More contradictions brought boldly together.

John Reed and Clive Wake write of the 'fulness of his [Seng-
hor's] cultural position, just as his theoretic writing on négritude postulates an ultimate all-inclusiveness in the concept of
the Culture of the Universal'. Within the confidence of this
position, which was hard-won for a black man between two
worlds, Senghor could write a poem like the one I have quoted.
He fought in the French Army and was imprisoned by the Ger-
mans in the war against the Nazis. The discriminatory treatment by the French of his fellow Senegalese soldiers inspired
some of his best poetry; at the same time, as Reed and Wake
write, 'War confirms Senghor's loyalty to France'; and his spirit
is able to make of that a finding of a 'new solidarity with his
own people and also with the common people of France'. He
made no excuses for his attachment to Europe and a European
religion, and did not allow these to become a threat to his commitment to Africa. This remarkable ability to synergise has
served in extension to his personal and particular conversion to
Marxism. As Claude Wauthier remarks, Senghor reconciled
'the humanist aspect of Marx's thinking with his own religious

convictions'. And, I would add, with the needs of the African
ethos to consider ways to appropriate the industrialised world.

As a South African, I naturally have a particular interest in
Senghor's play, *Chaka,* based on one of the earliest imaginative
interpretations of African history and heroes to be written by a
black, a kind of founding document, certainly, of our South
African literature—Thomas Mofolo's novel *Chaka.* Chaka is a
towering figure whose shadow will continue to fall many ways
over the struggle against colonialism, from its beginnings as military conquest resisted in the era of Chaka, to the tactics of modern guerrilla armies such as South Africa's *Umkhonto weSizwe* and
civilian mass action. Chaka was a cruel despot, he even killed his
own wife, Noliwe: Senghor has been accused of not condemning,
in his play, Chaka's brutality, but his interpretation of Chaka's
killing of his beloved wife may also be understood as symbolic of
the terrible ultimate sacrifice of *all that is personal* demanded by a
struggle for freedom. Claude Wauthier says, 'Senghor sees Chaka
as a forerunner of African unity, a visionary who wanted to prepare for the fight against the white invader.'

Senghor's writing, for those of us who lived far from his
complementary political life, was a source in the cultural struggle that contributed, with an essential spirit, to the liberation
struggle in South Africa. Now there is a new phase of liberation
to be sought in our country. The need for reconciliation of cultures. Here, in his life and writings, Senghor is a pioneer. At the
first Congress of African Writers and Artists in 1956 he said,
'We are all cultural half-castes'. But his life has revised and
refuted that definition. 'Half-caste' posits a diminition of one
blood, one identity, its dilution by another. He proves that it is
possible to keep your own culture and identity intact while
fully appropriating another; while participating widely, opening yourself to thought-systems, ideas, mores, of other peoples.

He is not a black Frenchman. He is perhaps the most successful example of cultural wholeness achieved in Africa in a single individual. It is surely something to be celebrated; for Africa cannot cast off the world culturally, economically, ecologically, any more than Europe, the Americas and Asia can cast off Africa in any of these ways. It is an ideal that underlies the extraordinary political and social initiative headed by that other man of the century, Nelson Mandela, in our own country: in its generalized, pragmatic form it is the determination to achieve a nonracial democracy in the not-so-easy circumstances of an African country that has a sizeable population of people who have been given the right to declare themselves as nothing other than White Africans.

Senghor has come all the way; we others have the cultural synthesis still to make. None expresses the ideal fulfilment of it better than he:

> *. . . unity is rediscovered, the reconciliation of*
> *the Lion the Bull and the Tree,*
> *the idea is linked to the act, the ear to the*
> *heart, the sign to the sense.*

GÜNTER GRASS

———◦◦◦———

*I*n our time the destiny of man presents its meaning in political terms.

So wrote Thomas Mann.

When Günter Grass and I were talking together last year, he said, 'My professional life, my writing, all the things that interest me, have taught me that I cannot freely choose my subjects. For the most part, my subjects were assigned to me by German history, by the war that was criminally started and conducted, and by the never-ending consequences of that era. Thus my books are fatally linked to these subjects, and I am not the only one who has had this experience.'

The destiny of the man or the woman as a writer is to open up, explore, illuminate the inescapable destiny of our time of which Thomas Mann wrote. No writer of the twentieth century who has come after Mann's generation has fulfilled this destiny better than Günter Grass. Not only in Germany, but in the world.

While the television pictures of war in the streets and celebrations in the palaces flash by and the newspaper headlines are pulped for recycling, the dog Prinz, the Flounder, and the Toad—they are seers of the *consequences* of events, the past that is never over.

The Snail is the ikon of our slow and painful trail when, as Günter's companion in great achievement, Bertolt Brecht, says: 'The travails of the mountains lie behind us./Before us lie the travails of the plains.' Oskar, from under the skirts of the past, misses nothing of what the world is making of itself for the future.

Genius is always controversial, no matter in what context it occurs. The iconoclasm of painters who rearrange the perceptions of the eye is attacked from whatever is the current conservatism—abstraction, conceptualism, neo-expressionism, whatever. In literature, for the writer as for the painter, there is the same basic imperative: we have to find the way to 'say' in our medium, what can deal with, express our time in its particularity and in its place fatally roped to human history.

Günter Grass not only has brought a formidable intellect to the political meaning of human destiny—his own life shaped by it in the dire twentieth-century manifestations of war and social engineering. He has found, for himself, in his writing the richly discursive, expansive mode, the ironic humour, the inverse tenderness, the chaos become a kind of order, the *fantastic character* of ordinary life in times when brutality is everyday and lies are retold often enough to become that apparently outdated definition, truth.

He is one of those rare writers who have changed the possibilities of fiction. Made it perform anew. While many literary critics credit Gabriel García Márquez with this, it was and is Günter Grass who exploded contemporary fiction and discovered new spaces, new freedom for the imagination as it transforms the thin representation of life that is fact.

It is not his stylistic innovation in the imaginative re-creation of reality that has made him controversial, however; indeed, that has inspired a number of writers, widely dispersed, who derive from him. He has been and remains controversial because he has not and never will accept substitute definitions of the truth—for then, and now; for what was East, and what still is West, at home in Germany, and in the world. In his latest writings, as in the work he has splendidly achieved during the whole of his three-score-and-ten-years, his genius is still going out after the truth, he is in pursuit. And that is what is noble, in the life of a writer and a human being; that quest is his *reputation*, which cannot be soiled by the slavering and yelping of any media-man.

Günter Grass is a modern Renaissance phenomenon. Even if he had not been a writer, his paintings and sculpture would have distinguished him with high originality, passion, and wit. While exploring the political destiny of our century he has a loving awareness of the natural world in whose context all destinies are played. There's a consequent wholeness to his vision; I was enchanted to find it symbolised in a small incident when, showing me water-colours of the countryside into which he had painted poetry, he called this his *aquadichte*, translated for me into English as 'aquarhyme'.

I have been lucky enough to get to know Günter personally, but even if I had never met him I would have come, as I have now, thousands of kilometres to celebrate him, because his writings have roused in me fresh responses and understanding of this strange century, now passing into history with all its ugly sins, he and I have inhabited.

—Günter Grass seventieth-birthday celebration
Hamburg, 1997

THE DIALOGUE OF
LATE AFTERNOON

———◦———

I have visited Egypt three times in my life and have never met Naguib Mahfouz. The first times, 1954 and 1958, I had not heard of him or his work; by the third time, 1993, all his work available in English translation was deeply familiar to me and counted, in my canon, as part of the few great international contemporary literary achievements. In 1993 I had asked my kind hosts to arrange for us to meet, but in their zeal to make me welcome they planned for this to happen at a large gathering with other Egyptian writers, and Naguib Mahfouz, by temperament and in the deserved privacy of old age, does not attend such public events. My days in Cairo were few and there was not time to seek another opportunity. It does not matter. The essence of a writer's being is in the work, not the personality, though the world values things otherwise, and would rather see what the writer looks like on television than read where he or she really is to be found: in the writings.

I am inclined to believe that a similar valuation may be applied to autobiography. The writer's gift to fellow humans is his or her gifts, the bounty of the creative imagination which comes from no-one knows where or why. The persona of the writer is the vessel. Whether it is flamboyantly decorated by a life-style of excess in alcoholism, adventurism, sexual experiment, or whether it is sparsely chased by what appears to be domestic dullness, its content has been poured into the work; the truth of it is there. (Sometimes in spite of the author . . .) Of course there are exceptions, but in general fiction writers who produce autobiographies are those whose autobiographies are better than their novels. Which has something to indicate about the limitation of their gifts. Let the biographers trace the chronology of life from the circumstances of the birth to the honoured or forgotten grave. What that span produced is already extant, transformed, freed from place and time.

The aphorisms, parables, allegories in the latest work of Naguib Mahfouz, *Echoes of an Autobiography*, have no dates appended. It's of no account when he wrote them. The back-and-forth of a mind creating its consciousness expands and contracts, rather than roves between past and present, with a totality which is not merely memory. Indeed, with the wry humour that flashes through profundity in all his thinking, Mahfouz meets memory as 'an enormous person with a stomach as large as the ocean, and a mouth that could swallow an elephant. I asked him in amazement, "Who are you, sir?" He answered with surprise, "I am forgetfulness. How could you have forgotten me?" ' The *totality* is comprehension of past and present experience as elements which exist contemporaneously. These pieces are meditations which echo that which was, has been, and is the writer Mahfouz. They are—in the words of the title of one of its prose pieces— 'The Dialogue of Late Afternoon' of his life. I don't believe any autobiography, with its inevitable implication of self-presentation, could have matched what we have here.

If the prose pieces in *Echoes of an Autobiography* have no dates they do each have a title, and these in themselves are what one might call the *essence of the essence* of Mahfouz's discoveries in and contemplation of life. The preoccupations so marvellously explored in his fiction appear almost ideographically, the single word or phrase standing for morality, justice, time, religion, memory, sensuality, beauty, ambition, death, freedom. And all these are regarded through a changing focus: narrowing briefly to cynical; taking the middle distance of humour and affection; opening wide to reverence. Prompted by his own words— another title, 'The Train of the Unexpected'—I take the liberty of paraphrasing myself in what I have remarked elsewhere of Mahfouz: he has the gift of only great writers to contemplate all the possibilities inherent in life rather than discard this or that awkwardness for consistency. The stimulus of his writing comes from the conflict of responses he elicits.

In 'A Man Reserves a Seat' a bus from a working-class suburb and a private car from a wealthy one set out for Cairo's station at the same moment, and arrive at the same time, colliding in an accident in which both are slightly damaged. But a man passing between the two is crushed and dies. 'He was crossing the Square to book a seat on the train going to Upper Egypt.' As one reads this laconic concluding sentence, almost an aside, the title suddenly leaps out, heavy type, in all the complexity of the many meanings it may carry. I read it thus: rich and poor arrive at the same point in human destiny whatever their means. Even the man who travels with neither, seeking to pass between the two, cannot escape; you cannot reserve a seat in destiny. There is no escape from the human condition, the final destination of which is death.

Naguib Mahfouz is an old man and it would be natural for him to reflect on that destiny/destination, inescapable for believers and unbelievers alike. But those of us who know his work know that he always has had death in mind as part of what life itself is. We are all formed by the social structures which are the corridors through which we are shunted and it is a reflection of the power of bureaucracy, the Egyptian civil service as regulator of existence and the height of ambition for a prestigious career, that his allegory of death should be entitled 'The Next Posting'. The question with which the allegory ends is one he may be asking himself now, but that he has contemplated for his fictional characters much earlier: 'Why did you not prepare yourself when you knew it was your inevitable destiny?' It is said—perhaps *he* has said, although he takes care to evade interviews and 'explanations' of his work—that Marcel Proust has influenced him. 'Shortly Before Dawn', 'Happiness', and 'Music' are disparate encounters in old age, where we shall not be recognizable to one another, as in the final gathering at the end of *A la Recherche du Temps Perdu*, but the mood is un-Proustian in the compensation that something vivid remains from what one has lost. In 'Music' the singer has been forgotten but the *tawashih* music she sang is still a delight. Life takes up the eternal, discards the temporal.

Politics: almost as inevitable as death, in account of a lifetime in Mahfouz's span and ours, children of the twentieth century. The morality of politics is intricately and inextricably knotted to the morality of personal relations in Mahfouz's masterpiece, *The Cairo Trilogy*, and in some of his lesser works. In 'Layla' (the title is the woman's name in a tale in *Echoes of an Autobiography*) sexual morality is another strand. 'In the days of the struggle of ideas' Layla was a controversial figure. 'An aura of beauty and allurement' surrounded her and while some saw her as a liberated pioneer of freedom, others criticised her as nothing but an immoral woman. 'When the sun set and the struggle and ideas disappeared from sight . . . many emigrated . . . Years later they returned, each armed with a purse of gold and a cargo of disrepute.' Layla laughs, and enquires, 'I wonder what you have to say now about immorality?' The essential question 'When will the state of the country be sound?' is answered: 'When its people believe that the end result of cowardice is more disastrous than that of behaving with integrity.' But this politico-moral imperative is not so easy to follow. In a political dispute ('The Challenge') a minister in government is asked, 'Can you show me a person who is clean and unsullied?', and the answer comes: 'You need but one example of many—the children, the idiotic, and the mad—and the world's still doing fine!'

Again, Mahfouz's surprise about-face startles, flipping from biting condemnation to—what? Irony, cynicism, accusatory jeers at ourselves? Or is there a defiance there? The defiance of survival, if not 'doing fine' morally, then as expressed by the courtesan in 'Question and Answer' who says, 'I used to sell love at a handsome profit, and I came to buy it at a considerable loss. I have no other choice with this wicked but fascinating life.' In 'Eternity' one of the beggars, outcast sheikhs, and blind men who wander through Mahfouz's works as the elusive answer to salvation, says, 'With the setting of each sun I lament my wasted days, my declining countries, and my transitory gods.' It is a cry of mourning for the world that Mahfouz sounds here; but not an epitaph, for set against it is the perpetuation, no choice, of this 'wicked but fascinating life'.

At a seminar following a lecture I gave on Mahfouz's *Cairo Trilogy* at Harvard a few years ago some feminists attacked his depiction of women characters in the novel; they were outraged at the spectacle of Amina, Al-Sayid Ahmad Abd al-Jawal's wife, forbidden to leave the family house unless in the company of her husband, and at the account of the fate of the girls in the family, married off to men of Jawal's choice without any concern for their own feelings, and without the possibility of an alternative independent existence. The students were ready to deny the genius of the novel on these grounds. It was a case of killing the messenger: Mahfouz was relaying the oppression of Amina and her daughters as it existed; he was not its advocate. His insight to the complex socio-sexual mores, the seraglio-prison that distorted the lives of women members of Jawal's family, was a protest far more powerful than that of those who accused him of literary chauvinism.

In this present echo of the values of Mahfouz's lifetime, woman is the symbol not only of beauty and joy in being alive but also of spiritual release. This is personified as, in celebration, not male patronage, 'a naked woman with the bloom of the nectar of life' who has 'the heart of music as her site'. The Proustian conception (let us grant it, even if only in coincidence with Mahfouz's own) of love as pain/joy, inseparably so, also has a Mahfouzian wider reference as a part of the betrayal by time itself, let alone any lover. Entitled 'Mercy', the aperçu reflects on an old couple: 'They were brought together by love thirty years ago, then it had abandoned them with the rest of expectations.'

Love of the world, 'this wicked but fascinating life', is the dynamism shown to justify itself as essential to religious precepts sometimes in its very opposition to them. The greed for life is admissible to Mahfouz in all his work; against which, of course, there is juxtaposed *excess as unfulfilment*. Yet how unashamedly joyous is the parable of 'The Bridegroom': 'I asked Sheik Abd-Rabbih al-Ta'ih about his ideal among those people with whom he had been associated, and he said: "A good man whose miracles were manifested by his perseverance in the ser-

vice of people and the remembrance of God; on his hundredth
birthday he drank, danced, sang, and married a virgin of
twenty. And on the wedding night there came a troop of angels
who perfumed him with incense from the mountains of Qaf at
the end of the earth." '

It is detachment that sins against life. When the narrator
tells the Sheikh, 'I heard some people holding against you your
intense love for the world', the Sheikh answers, 'Love of the
world is one of the signs of gratitude, and evidence of a craving
for everything beautiful.' Yet this is no rosy denial that life is
sad: 'It has been decreed that man shall walk staggeringly
between pleasure and pain.' Decreed by whom? The responsibility for this is perhaps aleatory, cosmic rather than religious,
if one may make such a distinction? And there is the question of
mortality, since nowhere in these stoic but not materialist writings is there expressed any belief in after-life, or any desire for
it; paradise is not an end for which earthly existence is the
means. This life, when explored and embraced completely and
fearlessly by tender sceptic and obdurate pursuer of salvation
Naguib Mahfouz, is enough. Mortality becomes the Sheikh's
serene and exquisite image: 'There is nothing between the lift-
ing of the veil from the face of the bride and the lowering of it
over her corpse but a moment that is like a heartbeat.' And after
a premonition of death one night, all the Sheikh asks of God,
instead of eternal life, is 'well-being, out of pity for people who
were awaiting my help the following day.'

If sexual love and sensuality in the wider sense of all its
forms is not an element opposed to, apart from, spirituality,
there is at the same time division *within that acceptance*, for life
itself is conceived by Mahfouz as a creative tension between
desires and moral precepts. On the one hand, sensuality is the
spirit of life, life-force; on the other, abstinence is the required
condition to attain spirituality.

It is said that Mahfouz has been influenced by Sufism. My own acquaintance with Sufism is extremely superficial, confined to an understanding that its central belief is that the awakening to the inner life of man is a necessary condition of fulfilment as a human being, while both the outer and inner realities are inseparable. Readers like myself may receive Sufism through the transmission of Mahfouz as, for precedent, anyone who is not a Christian may receive Christian beliefs in the *Pensées*: through Pascal. (And by the way, there is a direct connection there, between the paths of the Sufi and the Christian. Pascal: 'To obtain anything from God, the external must be joined to the internal.') Faith, no matter what its doctrine, takes on the contours of individual circumstance, experience, and the meditation upon these of the adherent. We therefore may take manifestations of Sufi religious philosophy that are to be discerned in Mahfouz's thinking as more likely to be his own gnosis, original rather than doctrinal. There is surely no heresy in this; only celebration of the doubled creativity: a resplendent intelligence applied to the tenets of what has to be taken on faith.

If we are to take a definitive reading of where Mahfouz stands in relation to faith, I think we must remember what his most brilliantly conceived character, Kamal, has declared in *The Cairo Trilogy*: 'The choice of a faith still has not been decided. The great consolation I have is that it is not over yet.' For Mahfouz, life is a search in which one must find one's own signposts. The text for this is his story 'Zaabalawi'. When a sick man goes on a pilgrimage through ancient Cairo to seek healing from the saintly Sheikh Zaabalawi, everybody he asks for directions sends him somewhere different. Told at last he will find the saint (who is also dissolute: see unity-in-dichotomy, again) in a bar, the weary man falls asleep waiting for him to appear. When he wakes, he finds his head wet. The drinkers tell him Zaabalawi came while he was asleep and sprinkled water on him to refresh him. Having had this sign of Zaabalawi's existence, the man will go on searching for him all his life—'Yes, I have to find Zaabalawi.'

The second half of the prose in the present collection is devoted to the utterances and experiences of another Sheikh, one Abd-Rabbih al-Ta'ih, who as his spokesman is perhaps Naguib Mahfouz's imagined companion of some of the saintly sages in Sufi history, such as Rabi'a al-Adawiya (a woman) of Basra, Imam Junayd al-Baghdadi of Persia, Khwaja Mu'in'ud-Din Chisti of India, Sheikh Muzaffer of Istanbul. He is also, surely, Zaabalawi, and brother of all the other wanderers who appear and disappear to tantalize the yearning for meaning and salvation in the streets of Mahfouz's works, offering and withdrawing fragments of answer to the mystery of existence, and guidance of how to live it well. This one, when first he makes his appearance in the quarter of Cairo invented for Mahfouz's notebooks, is heard to call out: 'A stray one has been born, good fellows.' The essence of this stray one's teaching is in his response to the narrator, Everyman rather than Mahfouz, who gives as his claim to join the Sheikh's Platonic cave of followers, 'I have all but wearied of the world and wish to flee from it.' The Sheikh says, 'Love of the world is the core of our brotherhood and our enemy is flight.'

One of the Sheikh's adages is: 'The nearest man comes to his Lord is when he is exercising his freedom correctly.' Many of Mahfouz's parables are of the intransigence of authority and the hopelessness of merely petitioning the powers of oppression. With the devastating 'After You Come Out of Prison' one can't avoid comparison with Kafka, although I have tried to do so since Kafka is invoked to inflate the false profundity of any piece of whining against trivial frustrations. In answer to a journalist's question, 'What is the subject closest to your heart?'

Mahfouz gave one of the rare responses in his own person: 'Freedom. Freedom from colonization, freedom from the absolute rule of kings, basic human freedom in the context of society and family. These types of freedom follow one from the other.' This love of freedom breathes from every line in this book. It is imbued with what his character Kamal has called 'a struggle towards truth aiming at the good of mankind as a whole . . . life would be meaningless without that' and with the tolerance Kamal's friend Husayn has defined: 'The Believer derives his love for these values from religion, while the free man loves them for themselves.'

Whatever your personal hermeneutics, it is impossible to read Mahfouz's work without gaining, with immense pleasure and in all gratitude, illumination through a quality that has come to be regarded as a quaint anachronism in modern existence, where information is believed to have taken its place. I pronounce with hesitation: Wisdom. Mahfouz has it. It dangles before us a hold on the mystery. Mahfouz is himself a Zaabalawi.

—1996

JOSEPH ROTH: LABYRINTH OF

EMPIRE AND EXILE

I approach writing about Joseph Roth's work somewhat defensively. Pundits will say I have no right because I admit I have no German and cannot read it in the original. How could I deny this lack, a deafness to what must be the bass and treble of his use of language? But I believe I have understood him according to my time and background. A writer whose work lives must be always subject to such a process—that is what keeps the work alive.

Strangely, while I have been writing this, the wheel of Karma—or historical consequence?—has brought Roth's territory back to a re-enactment of the situation central to his work.

In Roth we see a society—an empire—in which disparate nationalities are forced into political unity by an over-riding authority and its symbol: the Austro-Hungarian Empire and the personality of Emperor Franz Josef. There, the various grouped nationalities' restless rebellion, the rise of socialism and fascism against royalism, led to Sarajevo and the First World War. After the Second World War the groups that had won autonomy were forced together again, if in a slightly different conglomerate, by another all-powerful authority and its symbol: the Communist bloc and the personality of Joseph Stalin. Now restlessness and rebellion, this time against the socialism that has not proved to be liberation, bring once again the breakup of a hegemony. Passages in Roth's work, about the Slovenes, Croats, and Serbs, could with scarcely a change describe what has happened in Yugoslavia in 1991.

Roth: he looks out from a book-jacket photograph. Just the face in a small frame; it is as if someone held up a death mask. The ovals of the eyes are black holes. The chin pressed up against the black shadow of a moustache hides stoically the secrets of the lips. A whole life bronzed there. And there's another image in that face: the sight of the huge sightless eyes with their thick upper and lower lids dominating the width of the face has the mysteriously ancient gaze of a foetus, condemned to suffer the world.

'*Je travaille, mon roman sera bon, je crois, plus parfait que ma vie*', Roth wrote. Prefaces to some translations of his books give the same few penny-life facts: born in 1894 in Galicia, served in the Austro-Hungarian Army during the First World War, worked as a journalist in Vienna, Berlin, and Prague, left for France in 1933, wrote fifteen novels and novellas mainly while a figure in émigré opposition to the Nazis, died in Paris an alcoholic in 1939. I failed to find a full biography in English. After having re-read all Roth's fiction available to me, I am glad that, instead, I know him the only way writers themselves know to be valid for an understanding of their work: the work itself. Let the schools of literary criticism, rapacious fingerlings, resort to the facts of the author's life before they can interpret the text . . .

Robert Musil, Roth's contemporary in Austro-Hungary, although the two great writers evidently never met, put into the mouth of his Ulrich: 'One can't be angry with one's own time without damage to oneself'; to know that Roth's anger destroyed him, one has only to read the great works it produced. The text gives us the man, not t'other way about. The totality of Joseph Roth's work is no less than a *tragédie humaine* achieved in the techniques of modern fiction. No other contemporary writer, not excepting Thomas Mann, has come so close to achieving the wholeness—lying atop a slippery pole we never stop trying to climb—Lukács cites as our impossible aim. From the crude beginnings in his first novels, *The Spider's Web* (1923) and *Hotel Savoy* (1924), the only work in which Roth was satisfied to use the verbal equivalent of the expressionist caricaturing of a Georg Grosz or Otto Dix, through *Flight Without End* (1927), *The Silent Prophet* (1928?), and all his other works with, perhaps, the exception of the novellas *Zipper and His Father* (1928) and *Fallmerayer the Stationmaster* (1933), his anti-heroes are almost without exception soldiers, ex-prisoners of war, deserters: former aristocrats, bourgeois, peasants, and criminals all declassed in the *immorality* of survival of the 1914–18 war. This applies not only to the brutal or underhand necessity survival demands, but also to the sense that, in the terrible formulation of a last member of the Trotta dynasty, they had been 'Found unfit for death'.

All the young are material for the solutions of Communism or Fascism as the alternatives to despair or dissipation. Their fathers are unable to make even these choices, only to decay over the abyss of memory. All, young and old, are superfluous men to an extent Lermontov could not have conceived. Women are attendant upon them in this circumstance. Roth, although he often shows a Joycean transference in being able to write about women from under their skin, sees them in terms of their influence on men. 'We love the world they represent and the destiny they mark out for us.' While his women are rarely shown as overtly rejecting this male-determined solution to their existence, they are always unspokenly convinced of their entitlement to life, whether necessity determines it should be lived behind a bar, in a brothel bed, or as an old *grande dame* in poverty. No better than the men, they connive and plot; but even when he shows them at their slyest and most haughtily destructive, he grants them this spiritedness. Reading the life (his) from the work, it is evident that Roth suffered in love and resented it; in most of his work, desired women represent sexual frustration, out of reach.

The splendid wholeness of Roth's *oeuvre* is achieved in three ways. There's the standard one of cross-casting characters from one novel to the next. There's the far bolder risk-taking, in which he triumphs, of testing his creativity by placing different temperaments from different or (even more skilled) similar background in the same circumstances in different novels. There's the overall paradoxical unity of traditional opposition itself, monarchic/revolutionary, pitched together in the dissolution of all values, for which he finds the perfect physical metaphor: the frontier between Franz Josef's empire and the Tsar's empire, exemplified in Jadlowsky's tavern where Kapturak hides the Russian deserters he's going to sell to America and Australia. The only contacts between men are contraband; this commerce is the kind that is all that will be left of the two monarchic empires fighting each other to a mutual death, and the only structures that will still exist in the chaos to follow, and the early twentieth-century class struggle to arise from that.

Roth's *petite phrase* in the single great work into which all this transforms is not a Strauss waltz but the Radetzky March.

Its tempo beats from the tavern through Vienna and all the villages and cities of Franz Josef's empire, to those novels set in Berlin, where the other imperial eagle has only one head. For Roth's is the frontier of history. And it is not re-created from accounts of the past, as *War and Peace* was, but recounted contemporaneously by one who lived there, in every sense, himself. This is not an impudent literary value judgment; it is, again, the work providing a reading of the author's life. Here was a writer obsessed with and possessed by his own time. From within it he could hear the drum-rolls of the past resounding to the future.

Musil's evocation of that time is a marvellous discourse; Roth's is a marvellous evanescing of the author in his creation of a vivid population of conflicting individuals expressing that time. His method is a kind of picaresque struggling on the inescapable chain of the state. He rarely materializes authorially. There is his odd epilogue to *Zipper and His Father*, apparently some sort of acknowledgement that this, his most tender book (for while their situation makes both Musil and Roth ironic, Roth is tender where Musil is detachedly playful), is a form of the obeisance to the past that is autobiography. And there is his prologue to *The Silent Prophet*, his most politically realistic and least imaginatively realized book. In this prologue he comes as near as he ever will to an authorial credo in respect of his pervasive theme, the relation of the individual to the state. He says his characters are not 'intended to exemplify a political point of view—at most it (a life story) demonstrates the old and eternal truth that the individual is always defeated in the end.' The state/empire is the leg-iron by which his characters are grappled. The political movement against the state, with the aim of freeing the people, in Roth forges a leg-iron of its own by which the revolutionary individual is going to find himself hobbled.

Roth manages to convey complicated political concepts without their vocabulary of didacticism, rhetoric, and jargon. In the bitter experiences of Franz in *Flight Without End*, disillusion with the revolutionary Left conveys what must have been the one-time revolutionary Roth's own experience more tellingly than any research into his life could, and points to the paradox that runs through his novels with such stirring dialectical effect on the reader. The old royalist, capitalist, hierarchic world of church-and-state, with kings become divine authority on earth, their armies a warrior sect elected to serve as the panoply of these gods, is what he shows ruthlessly as both obsolete and blood-thirsty. But the necessary counter-brutality of the revolution, and the subsequent degeneration of its ideals into stultifying bureaucracy—surely a characterising tragedy of the twentieth century—leads him to turn about and show in his old targets, fathers, mothers, the loyalist, royalist land-owners and city fathers, enduring values in the very mores he has attacked.

This is hardly a synthesis for his dazzling fictional dialectic. One who came after him, Czeslaw Milosz, expresses the dilemma: 'Ill at ease in the tyranny, ill at ease in the republic, in the one I longed for freedom, in the other for the end of corruption.' After another world war and during some terrible regional ones, the collapse of ideologies and the emergence of new fanaticisms, have we now, too, nothing better to turn to than the conservatisms of the past? It troubles me that the writers whom I tend to admire most—Roth, Kundera, Milosz, Levi, Kiš—are those who reject, out of their own experience, the Left to which I remain committed in hope of its evolution. Perhaps it is because writers are better writers when they take the (selfish?) freedom of ignoring any constraints of loyalty? Or does their quality come from the unbearable freedom of exile—no plagiarism intended . . . This, which the others with the exception of Primo Levi share with Roth, provides the distancing, the slow rupture of membranes that is the ultimate strength of disillusion. Irrational, despised, and indispensable ties of home and habit which persist torturingly in inappropriate circumstances, in their characters, and make these powerless, become creative power in the writers themselves. Roth is a supreme exponent.

The ten years 1928–38 seem to mark the peak of Roth's mastery, although the dating of his novels, in terms of when they were written rather than when they were published, is often uncertain, since in the upheavals of exile some were not published chronologically. *The Radetzky March* (1932), *Weights and Measures* (1937), and *The Emperor's Tomb* (1938) are both the culmination of the other novels and the core round which they are gathered to form a manifold and magnificent work. *Zipper and His Father* (1928) and *Fallmerayer the Stationmaster* (1933) are a kind of intriguing coda, a foray into yet another emotional range, suggesting the kind of writer Roth might have become in another age, living another kind of life. Not that one would wish him any different.

Roth was a Jew in a time of growing persecution that drove him into exile, but as a writer he retained, as in relation to politics, his right to present whatever he perceived. Jewish tavern-keepers on the frontier fleece deserters. There is a wry look at Jewish anti-Semitism. In *Flight Without End* a university club has a *numerus clausus* for Jews carried out by Jews who have gained entry, and in *Right and Left*—a novel Roth seems to have written with bared teeth, sparing no-one—there is a wickedly funny portrait of the subtleties of Jewish snobbism/anti-Semitism in Frau Bernstein, who, while concealing that she is Jewish, as soon as someone at dinner seems about to tell a joke, would 'fall into a gloomy and confused silence—afraid lest Jews should be mentioned'. But old man Zipper, like Manes Reisiger, the cabby in *The Emperor's Tomb,* is a man with qualities—kindness, dignity in adversity, humour, love of knowledge for its own sake—and, yes, endearing Jewish eccentricities and fantasies, portrayed with the fond ironic humour that was inherited, whether he was aware of it or not, by Isaac Bashevis Singer.

Fallmerayer, the country stationmaster's passion for a Polish countess who enters his humble life literally by accident (a collision on the railway line), is an exquisite love story. Its erotic tenderness would have had no place—simply would have withered—plunged in the atmosphere of Roth's prison camps or rapacious post-war Vienna and Berlin. It takes place in that era, but seems to belong to some intimate seclusion of the creative imagination from the cynicism and cold-hearted betrayals that characterize love between men and women in most of Roth's work. Helping to get the injured out of the wreckage, Fallmerayer comes upon a woman on a stretcher, in a silver-gray fur coat, in the rain. 'It seemed to the stationmaster that this woman . . . was lying in a great island of white peace in the midst of a deafening sea of sound and fury, that she even emanated silence.'

The central works, *The Radetzky March* and *The Emperor's Tomb*, are really one, each novel beautifully complete and yet outdoing this beauty as a superb whole. Jacket copy dubs them a saga, since they encompass four generations of one branch of the Trotta family in *Radetzky* and two collaterals in *The Emperor*. But this is no mini-series plodding through the generations. It is as if, in the years after writing *Radetzky*, Roth were discovering what he had opened up in that novel, and turned away from

with many dark entries, leading to still other entries, not ven-
tured into. There were relationships whose transformations he
had not come to the end of: he had still to turn them around to
have them reveal themselves to him in other planes of their
complexity. So it is that the situation between fathers and sons,
realized for the reader with the ultimate understanding of
genius in *Radetzky*, is revealed to have an unexplored aspect, the
situation between son and mother in *Emperor*. And this is no
simple mirror-image; it is the writer going further and further
into what is perhaps the most mysterious and fateful of all
human relationships, whose influence runs beneath and often
outlasts those between sexual partners. We are children and we
are parents: there is no dissolution of these states except death.

No theme in Roth, however strong, runs as a single current.
There are always others, running counter, washing over,
swelling its power and their own. The father/son, mother/son
relationship combines with the relationship of the collection of
peoples to a political determination laid as a grid across their
lives. And this itself is a combination with the phenomenon by
which the need for worship (an external, divine order of things)
makes an old man with a perpetual drip at the end of his nose,
Franz Josef, the Emperor-god; and, again, combines with an
analysis—shown through the life of capital city and village—of
an era carrying the reasons for its own end, and taking half the
world down with it.

'Though fate elected him [Trotta] to perform an outstanding
deed, he himself saw to it that his memory became obscured to
posterity.'

How unfailingly Roth knew how to begin! That is the
fourth sentence in *The Radetzky March*. His sense of the ridicu-

lous lies always in the dark mesh of serious matters. Puny opposition (an individual) to the grandiose (an empire); what could
have led to the perversity of the statement? And while following the novel the reader will unravel from this thread not simply how this memory was obscured, but how it yet grew
through successive generations and was transformed into a
myth within the mythical powers of empire.

The outstanding deed is not recounted in retrospect. We are
in the battle of Solferino and with Trotta, a Slovenian infantry
lieutenant, when he steps out of his lowly rank to lay hands
upon the Emperor Franz Josef and push him to the ground, taking in his own body the bullet that would have struck the
Emperor. Trotta is promoted and honoured. A conventional
story of heroism, suitable for an uplifting chapter in a school-
book; which it becomes. But Captain Joseph Trotta, ennobled
by the appended 'von Sipolje', name of his native village, has
some unwavering needle of truth pointing from within him.
And it agitates wildly when in his son's first reader he comes
upon a grossly exaggerated account of his deed as the Hero of
Solferino. In an action that prefigures what will be fully realized
by another Trotta, in time to come, in some of the most brilliant passages of the novel, he takes his outrage to the Emperor
himself, the one who surely must share with him the validity of
the truth. 'Look here, my dear Trotta,' said the Emperor, ' . . .
you know, neither of us shows up too badly in the story. Forget
it.' 'Your Majesty,' replied the Captain, 'it's a lie.'

Is honesty reduced to the ridiculous where 'the stability of
the world, the power of the law, and the splendour of royalty are
maintained by guile'? Trotta turns his back on his beloved
army, and estranged by rank and title from his peasant father,
vegetates and sourly makes of *his* son Franz a District Commissioner instead of allowing him a military career.

The third generation of Trottas is the District Commissioner's son, Carl Joseph, who, with Roth's faultless instinct for timing, enters the narrative aged fifteen to the sound of the Radetzky March being played by the local military band under his father's balcony. The D.C. has suffered a father withdrawn by disillusion; he himself knows only to treat his own son, in turn, in the same formula of stunted exchanges, but for the reader though not the boy, Roth conveys the sense of something withheld, longing for release within the D.C. Brooded over by the portrait of his grandfather, the Hero of Solferino, lonely Carl Joseph is home from the cadet cavalry school where he has been sent to compensate the D.C. for his own deprivation of military prestige. The boy is seduced by the voluptuous wife of the sergeant-major at the D.C.'s gendarmerie post. When she dies in childbirth, Carl Joseph, concealing his immense distress from his father, has to pay a visit of condolence to the sergeant-major, Slama, and is given by him the packet of love letters he wrote to the man's wife. 'This is for you, Herr Baron . . . I hope you'll forgive me, it's the District Commissioner's orders. I took it to him at once after she died.' There follows a wonderful scene in the dramatic narrative restraint Roth mastered for these later books. Devastated Carl Joseph goes into the village café for a brandy; his father is there and looks up from a newspaper. 'That brandy she gave you is poor stuff . . . Tell that waitress we always drink Hennessy.'

One has hardly breathed again after this scene when there is another tightening of poignantly ironic resolution. Father and son walk home together. Outside the door of the D.C.'s office is Sergeant Slama, helmeted, with rifle and fixed bayonet, his ledger under his arm. 'Good day, my dear Slama,' says Herr von Trotta. 'Nothing to report, I suppose.' 'No, sir,' Slama repeats, 'nothing to report.'

Carl Joseph is haunted by the portrait of the Hero of Solferino, and though himself inept and undistinguished in his military career, dreams of saving the Emperor's life as his grandfather did. A failure, haunted as well by the death of Slama's wife (Roth leaves us to draw our own conclusion that the child she died giving birth to may have been Carl Joseph's) and his inadvertent responsibility for the death of his only friend in a duel, Carl Joseph's only fulfilment of this dream is when, incensed by the desecration, he tears from the wall in a brothel a cheap reproduction of the official portrait of the Emperor—that other image which haunts his life. Roth reconceives this small scene in full scale when, at a bacchanalian ball that might have been staged by Fellini on a plan by Musil's Diotima for her 'Collateral Campaign' to celebrate Emperor Franz Josef's seventy-year reign, the news comes of the assassination of the Emperor's son at Sarajevo. Some Hungarians raucously celebrate: 'We all agree we ought to be glad the swine's done for.' Trotta, drunk, takes 'heroic' exception—'My grandfather saved the Emperor's life . . . I will not stand by and allow the dynasty to be insulted!' He is forced to leave ignominiously.

As the District Commissioner's son deteriorates through gambling and drink, Roth unfolds with marvellous subtlety what was withheld, longing for release in the father. The aged District Commissioner's unrealized bond with his old valet, Jacques, is perfectly conveyed in one of the two superlative set-pieces of the novel, when Jacques's dying is first merely a class annoyance because the servant fails to deliver the mail to the breakfast table, and then becomes a dissolution of class differences in the humanity of two old men who are all that is left, to one another, of a vanished social order: their life.

The second set-piece both echoes this one and brings back a scene that has been present always, beneath the consequences

that have richly overlaid it. The levelling of age and social dissolution respects no rank. The D.C. not only now is at one with
his former servant; he also, at the other end of the ancient order,
has come to have the same bond with his exalted Emperor. In an
audience recalling that of the Hero of Solferino, he too has gone
to ask for the Emperor's intercession. This time it is against
Carl Joseph's demission in disgrace from the army. The dodder-
ing Emperor says of Carl Joseph, ' "That's the young fellow I
saw at the last manoeuvres." Since this confused him a little, he
added, "You know, he saved my life. Or was that you?" A
stranger catching sight of them at this moment might have
taken them for brothers . . . the one felt he had changed into a
District Commissioner, the other, that he had changed into the
Emperor.' The unity of Roth's masterwork is achieved in that
highest faculty of the imagination Walter Benjamin speaks of
as 'an extensiveness of the folded fan, which only in spreading
draws breath and flourishes.'

Carl Joseph, firing on striking workers, hears them sing a
song he has never heard before. It is the *Internationale*. At the
same time, he has a yearning to escape to the peasant origins of
the Trotta family. Unable to retreat to the 'innocent' past,
superfluous between the power of the doomed empire and the
power of the revolution to come, he is given by Roth a solution
that is both intensely ironic and at the same time a strangely
moving assertion of the persistence of a kind of naked humanity, flagellated by all sides. Leading his men in 1914, he walks
into enemy fire to find something for them to drink. 'Lieutenant Trotta died, not with sword in hand but with two buck-
ets of water.'

Carl Joseph's cousin, of *The Emperor's Tomb*, has never met
him, although Roth knows how to give the reader a *frisson* by
casually dropping the fact that they were both in the battle at

which Carl Joseph was killed. But this Trotta does link with the peasant branch of the family, through his taking up, first as a form of radical chic, another cousin, Joseph Branco, an itinerant chestnut-roaster from Roth's familiar frontier town. Emotionally frozen between a mother who, like the D.C., cannot express her love, and a young wife who turns lesbian after he leaves her alone on their wedding night while he sits with a dying servant (the vigil of the D.C. with Jacques composed in a new key), this Trotta forms his warmest relationship with Branco and Branco's friend, the Jewish cabby. They go to war together, live together as escaped prisoners of war in Siberia, and in this phase of Roth's deepest reflection on the elements of his mega-novel, exemplify brilliantly his perception that consistency in human relations is not a virtue but an invention of lesser novelists. The ideal camaraderie of the three men cracks along unpredictable lines, just as the complexity of Trotta's love for and indifference to his wife, and her constant breaking out of what have seemed to be emotional resolutions to their life, are consonant with the jarring shifts of war and post-war that contain them. Like all Roth's work, this phase is wonderfully populous as any nineteenth-century novel, psychologically masterly, particularly in the person of Trotta's mother and the tangents of distress and illogical fulfilment in the relationship between him and her. But it was one of Roth's last works, published only the year before he died, the year the next war was preparing in his world, his time; although he wrote at least two more novels after this one, he concludes this phase, and—for me—the summation of his work, with Trotta in a café. On that night 'My friends' excitement seemed to me superfluous'—as it does to the reader, since it is not explained until, with Roth's power to shatter a scene with a blow of history, 'the moment when the door of the café flew open and an oddly dressed young man appeared on the threshold. He was in fact wearing black leather gaiters . . . and a kind of military cap which reminded me at one and the same time of a bedpan and a caricature of our old Austrian caps.'

The Anschluss has arrived. The café empties of everyone, including the Jewish proprietor. In an inspired fusion of form with content, there follows a dazedly disoriented piece of writing that expresses the splintering of all values, including emotional values, so that the trivial and accidental, the twitching involuntary, takes over. Trotta sits on in the deserted café, approached only by the watchdog. 'Franz, the bill!' he calls to the vanished waiter. 'Franz, the bill!' he says to the dog. The dog follows him in the dawn breaking over 'uncanny crosses' that have been scrawled on walls. He finds himself at the *Kapuzinergruft*, the Emperor's tomb, 'where my emperors lay buried in iron sarcophagi' . . . 'I want to visit the sarcophagus of my Emperor, Franz Josef . . . Long live the Emperor!' The Capuchin brother in charge hushes him and turns him away. 'So where could I go now, I, a Trotta?'

I know enough of the facts of Joseph Roth's life to be aware that he collapsed, for his own death, in a café, a station of exile's calvary.

AN EXCHANGE: KENZABURO OE,

NADINE GORDIMER

———⟫◆⟪———

4 April 1998

Dear Miss Gordimer,

I am reminding myself of the occasion of the visit you paid to Japan coming all the way from South Africa in the autumn of 1992. I took the underground to go and see you at your hotel in central Tokyo. On my way there my train passed the station that was to be the target of the indiscriminate sarin poisoning conducted by the terrorist leaders of the AUM Cult. The AUM incident was to be preceded earlier in the same year by the great earthquake which devastated another big city of Japan. You talk about it in your recent work *The House Gun* as an apocalyptic catastrophe along with the tragic incidents that took place in Bosnia and Somalia.

Naturally I had no premonition about the catastrophic incidents that were to happen here. But I was somehow sunk deep in melancholy. I was thinking of the modern history of South Africa which you initially experienced in your childhood and continually kept on representing in your novels and stories. In the beginning was the colonisation. It was followed by the establishment of apartheid, the long history of resistance against it, the victory of the organisation for the liberation of black Africans, and the release of Nelson Mandela. However, it was not a smooth progress towards liberation, freedom, and coexistence. On my way to your hotel I remembered the latest news by the foreign press of the attack on ordinary black citizens by the armed black forces, which resulted in as many as fifty deaths.

Waiting for my melancholic face, however, was your welcoming smile. While talking with you, I was relieved by the equipoise in which your intellectual profundity, emotional richness and empirical certitude were so well balanced. Our conversation took a humorous turn.

During our conversation I told you how impressed I was by and sympathised with the Preface to your Penguin edition of *Selected Stories* which I was reading on the underground. In your Preface you write: 'For everything one writes is part of the whole story, so far as any individual writer attempts to build the pattern of his own perception out of chaos: the story . . . will be complete with the last sentence written before one dies or imagination atrophies.' You also write: ' . . . in a certain sense a writer is "selected" by his subject—his subject being *the consciousness* of his era. How he deals with this is, to me, the fundament of commitment . . . '

It now comes home to me too that a writer spends his lifetime continuously in writing a story which comprehends the whole of his life in its entirety. A few years ago I made up my mind to give up writing novels and more directly to comprehend my own life and the age in which I lived. By doing so I meant to try, a little prematurely, to read the whole story built up of all the words and sentences I had written.

In a critical review of your new writing someone asked why you continue to deal with the social situations in South Africa. However, you had already answered the question with conviction. Like you I am now determined to continue to write, to the very last of the words I write, the subject selected by the age I live in, and I have resumed writing a novel.

Your most recent novel available in Japan is *My Son's Story*. I once discussed the opening of this novel: a leader of the liberation movement in South Africa who is 'coloured' and falls in love with his supporter, a white woman, who reciprocates; his wife, in the meantime, had become an active revolutionary, even before he knew about it, and was arrested. The white woman realised that she was not qualified to shed tears over the predicament of her lover's wife, caused by the wife's struggle for justice, because she, the white woman, had betrayed the wife by loving her husband. I emphasised that in this situation which was hard to bear she maintained her human integrity. Later I received a letter from someone who had been a student among the audience of my lecture at a women's college and was now married, with a baby, telling me that after having read through the whole novel in translation she was now able to understand what I had then said.

Recently in Japan a novel of 'infidelity' has been read so widely as to become a social phenomenon. Here, however, the theme of double suicide as the ultimate consequence of a love affair has tended to be contained in narratives of extremely narrow scope with no bearing on social situations. Very different from them is your novel which also deals with the theme of infidelity. In your *My Son's Story* the daughter is upset when she comes to know about her father's secret. She attempts to commit suicide. She gets over her predicament, however, and transforms herself by taking part in the liberation movement with her comrades. Her mother, too, through collaborating with her, comes to lead an entirely new life. She never flinches in the face of oppression. Further this brings about her father's regeneration as a leader. And the son comes to write a novel about the entire history of the whole family.

I sincerely hope that *My Son's Story* will be read by a larger audience in Japan. I wish that *The House Gun* also would be translated into Japanese as soon as possible. You deal with the theme of the new role of family and that of violence. These themes are most relevant to the Japanese consciousness of our era. You have been 'selected' by these themes and you tackle them with utmost sincerity.

One of the central social problems of present-day Japan is juvenile delinquency resorting to violence. A boy killed another boy, who was inferior physically as well as intellectually, and hung up the victim's head in public. On another occasion a middle-school boy stabbed his woman teacher to death with a knife. There have been a number of suicide cases as a result of the bullying of weaklings. An old man was beaten to death by two girls; a father killed by his son and his son's friend.

The mass media in Japan is busy dealing with these social phenomena in wide-ranging terms such as the personality of the juvenile delinquent, the state of local communities, the Juvenile Law, the national education system, etc.

More relevant to me as a writer is to deal with the problem as that of the inner psyche of these juvenile delinquents. It is characteristic of our age that when a symbolic or typical incident brings a cluster of problems to the surface, then, as if given stimulus to turn into an avalanche, similar kinds of incidents follow in its wake. I have once written to express my wish for the children to be restored to their normal selves with the power of self-respect inherent in them originally.

My remarks evoked the criticisms against me from a sometime school-teacher and writer of children's literature, and a woman actively engaged in running a circle of children and their mothers. They said: attention must be drawn not to the power inherent in children but to the external pressures that are driving them into difficulties; one must try to listen to their muted cries for help. I had to admit that they were right. Even so, I still hold that education, whether public or private, should be based on trusting the power of recovery inherent in children themselves.

We must be wary of the view gaining more ground and spreading widely: that responsible for children's bent towards violence are the Juvenile Law and the education system, which were both moulded under the democratic constitution after the end of World War II. According to this view even the *democratic idea* of the family is criticised. Such views are nothing but an unmistakable variation of the blatant neo-nationalism that has been aggrandising itself during the recent years in Japan.

I fear that such views will give rise to another avalanche in the mass media in Japan: tolerant laws that should protect juvenile 'rights' (even this word in Japanese is now used in a pejorative sense) will be turned into the ones that would bind them; schools would be furnished with equipment for containing violence; and the family would become a repressive institution. Children as a whole would then find themselves cornered even further.

Under such circumstances the family relationship in particular would see a grotesque re-emergence of undemocratic environment that I experienced as a child during World War II. You would come to consider, again, Japan and the Japanese 'different' or deviated from the norm. All this would no doubt disturb you in the Western world.

What then could specifically be done with the deplorable

state of violence occurring frequently in which some children prey upon other children or are preyed upon by them? As a writer (for the writer in many respects stands on the same side with children) I think as follows: now the whole world is covered with massive violence; children's bent towards violence in Japan is not a phenomenon unique to Japan; all the children of the world, in their perception and consciousness of their era, are the mirrors upon which that massive universal violence is reflected or are its miniature models. We grown-ups cannot segregate children and put them aside. We cannot but stand all on the same side, listen to all their cries for help, whether muted or amplified, and confront face to face the roots of violence. Only with such an essential shift of attitude on our part would the family, as a flexible instrument for children and grown-ups alike, be able to restore our true selves with the power inherent in us.

My reading of your novels has shaped these thoughts of mine. I am thus writing this letter in the hope that your answer will serve as the best possible encouragement for Japanese children and their parents.

> Yours sincerely,
> Kenzaburo Oe

Johannesburg, 18th April 1998

Dear Kenzaburo, (may we use our given names?)

Your letter brings the pleasure of realization that we are simply taking up from where we were interrupted by the end of our encounter in the Tokyo hotel six years ago. There was so much to exchange; it has existed, in the parentheses of our separate lives, ready to continue any time. The ambiguity, the connections that criss-cross against chronology between that short meeting and what was going to happen—an invisible prescience which would influence our individual thinking and writing—*that* turns out to have presaged the links of our *then* and *now*. You came to our meeting unknowingly in the fore-shadow of the terrible earthquake that was to devastate a Japa-nese city later that year, and that I was to use, in a novel as yet not conceived, as a metaphor for apocalyptic catastrophe wreaked by nature, alongside that of contemporary devastation by humans upon themselves in Eastern Europe and Africa.

And so now I should not have been surprised that you, writ-ing to me, are preoccupied by the question of violence entering deeply into your awareness, just as it has made its way into mine. This is a 'recognition' between two writers; but it goes further. It is the recognition of writers' inescapable need to read the signs society gives out cryptically and to try to make sense of what these really mean.

I must tell you that when I began to write *The House Gun* it came to me as the personal tragedy of a mother and father whose son, in a crime of passion, murders their human values along with the man he kills. The parallel theme, placing their lives in the context of their country, the new South Africa, was that they—white people who in the past regime of racial dis-crimination had always had black people dependent upon *them*—would find themselves dependent upon a distinguished black lawyer to defend their son. That was going to be the dou-ble thesis of my novel. But as I wrote (and isn't it always the way with us, our exploration of our story lures us further and further into the complexity of specific human existences?), I found that the context of mother, father, and son was not exis-tentially determined only geographically and politically; there was the question of the very air they breathed. Violence in the air; didn't the private act of *crime passionel* take place within unconscious sinister sanction: the public, social banalisation of violence?

You make the true and terrible observation 'all the children of the world, in their perception and consciousness of their era, are the mirrors upon which the massive universal violence is reflected'. You are rightly most concerned about the situation of children, and I'll come to that, but first I must comment on the extraordinary, blinkered attitude to violence which I have just recently been subjected to rather than encountered, in Europe and the United States.

Whenever I was interviewed, journalists would propose the question of violence in South Africa as an isolated phenomenon, as if street muggings, burglaries, campus 'date rapes', brawls resulting in serious injuries, and even death, between so-called fans at sports matches, were not part of everyday life in their countries.

Let me admit at once that South African cities have at present a high place on the deplorable list of those with the worst crime rate in the world. Some South American cities have been prominent on that list so long that this has come to be regarded cynically by the rest of the world as a national characteristic, a kind of folk custom rather than a tragedy. Conversely, South Africa's violent crime is seen as a *phenomenon of freedom*—interpreted among racists everywhere (and there are still plenty of them) as evidence that blacks should have been kept under white hegemony for ever.

The reasons for the rise of crime in South Africa, however, are not those of black people's abuse of freedom. They are our heritage from apartheid. What the world does not know, or chose not to know, was that during the apartheid regime from 1948, State violence was quotidian and rampant. To be victims of State violence was the way of life for black men, women, and children. Violence is nothing new to us; it was simply confined to daily perpetration against blacks. They were shut away outside the cities in their black townships at night, or permanently banished to ethnically-defined territory euphemistically known as 'home-lands', from where only male contract workers were allowed to come to the cities. This was how urban law-and-order was maintained. Violence, and the desperate devaluation of life it called forth, was out of sight. Now that the people of our country are free in their own country to seek work and homes wherever they please, they flock to the cities. But the cities were not built for them; there is no housing for such vast numbers, and their presence on the labour market has swelled the ranks of the unemployed enormously. Their home is the streets; hunger turns them, as it would most of us who deplore crime on full stomachs, to crime, and degradation degenerates into violence. These are the historical facts which make the reasons for violence in South Africa exceptional; economic development has a chance to deal with them to a significant extent, but not entirely.

As for the matter of guns as domestic possessions in South Africa, along with the house cat—while I was in the U.S.A. two schoolboys aged eleven and thirteen shot dead several classmates and their teacher, and while I was in Paris a schoolboy shot and killed his classmate. Why did these children have access to guns? Where did they get them? The American children took the guns from the house of their grandfather; the French child from that of his father. The guns were simply there, in these family homes, commonplace objects, evidently not kept under lock and key, if they had any legitimate place at all in household equipment. I've just read American statistics revealing that a gun in the house is forty-three times more likely to kill a member of the household than an intruder.

And now you tell me that a Japanese boy killed a companion and hung up the victim's head in public; a boy fatally stabbed his teacher; an old man was beaten to death by two girls, and a father was killed by his son and the son's friend.

This brings us to what is the ultimate responsibility of adults in your country, in mine, in the whole world: why could children cold-bloodedly kill? What has made them horrifically indifferent to the pain and death of others, so that they themselves are prepared to inflict these? What has happened to their 'tender years'?

Setting aside the particular experience of South Africa, I think the woman who challenged you, citing environmental causes—an environment created entirely by the power and will of adults—was correct. If you look back at your own childhood experience, Kenzaburo, and I look back at mine, surely we shall see how our morality, our humanity was distorted by the agenda of adults, something we had to struggle with and shed by our own efforts as we grew: a confirmation of your conviction that there is the 'power of recovery inherent in children themselves', yes. You were brain-washed—no less—into believing that the immortal worth of the Emperor was such that you must be prepared to kill yourself at his command. I was brainwashed—no less—into believing that my white skin gave me superiority and absolute authority over anyone of another colour.

Children are not subjected to this sort of evil conditioning today. Then what is it, in countries dedicated to peace and democracy, reformed in aversion to the authoritarian cruelties of the past, that makes violence acceptable to children? I know it's easy to lay responsibility on the most obvious—the visual media, television and certain electronic games, now also part of home furnishings. But the fact is that these household presences have become the third parent. They raise the child according to a set of values of equal influence to that of the biological parents. The power of the image has become greater than the word; you can tell a child that a bullet in the head kills, a knife in the heart kills. The child *sees* the 'dead' actor appear, swaggering in another role, next day. This *devaluation* of pain, with its consequent blunting of inhibitions against committing violence, has become, through the acts of glamorous gangsters, mortal-ray-breathing heroes of outer space, the daily, hourly formation of youthful attitudes. It is hauntingly clear to me that these children who kill do not have—it's like an atrophied faculty—the capacity to relate to pain and destruction experienced in the flesh of others. I think this is what has happened to the 'inner psyche of these juvenile delinquents' you speak of.

What can we do, all of us adults, to take up the responsibility to children to 'restore their normal selves', how rouse 'the power of self-respect inherent in them originally'?

If we place a large share of the blame for their condition upon the media, are we then advocating censorship? The idea is repugnant and frightening to me, who spent decades fighting censorship of information, literature, the arts, in my country. I have in mind something so difficult to bring about that it may seem naïve to mention it. Is it not possible that writers, actors, directors, and producers of these programmes that make violence acceptably banal could reconsider their own values? It is said in what is known as the 'entertainment industry'—it has also become a brain-washing industry—that the industry simply gives the public what it wants. But the public is long conditioned to want what the industry dictates. And why is that public so passive under this self-appointed authority? Is it because the visual media are the representation of much accepted adult behaviour? The violence in the air is the exhalation of our being?

You know—more telling, even, than any statement in your letter—years ago you made a remarkable implicit claim for the ability of children to restore the power of self-respect inherent in them. The children in your early story (in English translation entitled 'Prize Stock') are the ones in a remote Japanese village who, by their actions and attitudes, teach the adults that the black American airman who has fallen into their hands during the war is a human being, capable of emotional response and suffering. Taking your premise that the power of self-respect is inherent in children, this means that it also must *still exist*, dormant, in the substance of adult men and women. How shall we release this power of restoration in our present era and circumstances?

Kenzaburo, you did not know how much you were speaking for the end of our millennium when you once used these words: *Teach us to outgrow our madness.*

Sincerely,
Nadine

10 May 1998
Dear Nadine (please allow me to reciprocate using each other's given names)

Thank you very much indeed for your welcome reply. It has served to rescue me from the sense of helpless isolation from the whole world as well as from the Japanese society, to which I have recently been susceptible. Your letter reminds me of the same kind of encouragement that I experienced in watching on television the opening ceremony of the Winter Olympics held in Nagano, Japan, last February. The keynote of the ceremony was basically one of age-old nationalism. The ceremony reached its climax, however, when my friend Seiji Ozawa conducted Beethoven's Ninth Symphony in the provincial town of Nagano with its orchestra while simultaneously the singers sang in unison at a number of places—in Africa, China, etc., with the *Song of Joy* resounding all over the world.

Seiji did his best to conduct whole mankind on this planet to unity by overcoming the time-lag that would normally be unavoidable in satellite transmission. I was deeply struck by the determined conviction which I detected in his face. By determined conviction I mean his act of praying—he once told me that while engaged in the performance of music he would attain the feeling that he was praying.

Dear Nadine it was thoughtful of you to remind yourself of my *O Teach us to Outgrow our Madness*. I am grateful to you and alive to the poignancy attached to the phrase. For the title of my work I borrowed the phrase from W. H. Auden's poem. It constitutes a part of the 'voice of Man' uttered in the middle of the battle between the Japanese army and the Chinese guerrillas. This universal voice concludes as follows: 'Till, as the contribution of our star, we follow/The clear instructions of that justice, in the shadow/Of whose uplifting, loving and constraining power/All human reasons do rejoice and operate.'

Along with this prayer, which has not been fulfilled, I cannot but think of the sufferings that Seiji Ozawa himself experienced during the post-war period. A contemporary of mine, Seiji as a boy was brought up on the Chinese mainland.

As for the background of urban violence in the newly-born South Africa, you have traced it in the whole modern history that began with apartheid. Dear Nadine, I admire your insight and courage, in contrast to the inadequacy of the Japanese media searching ineffectively for the origin of juvenile violence in this country.

Many people here say that the present juvenile violence is the product of the post-war democracy, the family system based on it, and the educational system as an extension of these. Notably enough, nobody speaks of the historical process by which, from the beginning of modernisation, Japan perpetrated violence to the utmost in other parts of Asia for the sake of self-aggrandisement until the end of World War II, when the massive violence of nuclear weapons burnt down the two Japanese cities. It seems that people have failed to reflect upon how 'the violence in the air', in your words, has been engendered. People are failing to do what we soon did after the end of the War.

An objection will be readily raised that there is little bearing of the Nanking incident on the Japanese children of today. This is the situation which I find myself in. I, for one, assert that it would be an effective way of anti-violence education to think, together with children, how Japanese citizens as a whole could make up for the irredeemable violence committed by the state in the past. Adults will have to change before children; adults thereby will restore confidence that they *can* change—these could be the concrete plans to be put into practice both at home and at school.

When I, an undergraduate student of foreign literature, started my career as a writer, I embraced the following two fundamental principles. One was to recapture afresh what custom had bedimmed: all the lustre of either consciousness or sensibility. On looking back I realize that this was nothing but 'defamiliarisation' as defined by the Russian formalists. Not only the novelists but also the media have the obligation to show to adults as well as to children the heavy and weary weight of death, violence and pain that comes home to human existence.

Another of my principles was to attach primary importance to imagination. In those days my contention was that there was in ordinary Japanese no equivalent to 'imagination' either in English or French. It is urgently needed to investigate whether serious literature and writings in the mass media give expression adequate enough to evoke imagination about death, violence and pain.

You are particularly concerned about the colossal mass media targeting children as their audience and instead of making them feel the images of death and violence as reality, represent these images as something with which they could not be directly involved. As a result death, violence and pain become something commonplace in the consciousness and sensibility of children. Their imagination has been numbed.

Such a trend is explicitly evident in the representation of chaotic future society by means of the visual media and cartoons (accompanied by words) produced under its influence. However, the masterpieces in Utopian literature, from Thomas Moore through Zamiatin to George Orwell, were invariably concerned with the present in which they lived, suffered and entertained their hopes. In the images of a violent future world prevalent in the visual media are reflected the men and society common to the present world, as you have agreed with me, 'overshadowed by massive violence'.

In my first letter I also wrote that 'all the children of the world, in their perception and consciousness of their era, are mirrors upon which the massive universal violence is reflected or are its miniature models.' Children perceive 'the violence in the air' overshadowing the present age and are familiarised to representations of violence by the visual and various other media. Under the circumstances, how vulnerable they are! As regards their vulnerability I may put it another way by saying that they can easily be victimised and incite those who are willing to victimise them. They can at once be weaklings who are victims of violence and bullies who exert violence—against other children, against their family members, or even against themselves by means of suicide, as Dante depicts in Canto XIII of *Inferno*.

What then should we do? I know from experience, painstaking though it may be, that I could not avoid thinking of what I should do as a novelist. As I am sure that you will never misunderstand me, I do not in the least regard the writing profession as something of a privilege. I simply wish to restore confidence that, in this age of the endless expansion of the visual media, television, computer games, etc., the novel's apparently old-fashioned methods of representations have the power of 'defamiliarising' death, violence and pain and could play the role of revitalizing and developing imagination for that purpose.

Would it be possible at all for the novel to regain children and youths as readers? When I say this, I am conceiving of the novel not as mere verbalization of the visual media but as something that genuinely deserves its name. And I wish to regain the reader who will be reading this kind of novel with much wished-for intensity. Shall we ever succeed in doing this? It will not be very easy in this country. At the present moment the more ambitious publishers draw their attention to anything other than literature.

Still I wish to repeat that violence prevailing all over the world is a problem of modern history that we have inherited from the generation immediately before us. Are we allowed to bequeath it unsolved to the next generation? While knowing that we are exacerbating it, aren't we standing on the verge of giving up our responsibilities? Under these circumstances I think it will be an urgent matter to address to adult readers.

Dear Nadine, please forgive me for having kept talking of grim subjects. I have been doing so, however, in the hope that, even concerning the difficult realities, you will be returning to us an essentially bright and encouraging message which I have always discovered in your admirable writings.

Yours sincerely
Kenzaburo

Johannesburg, 15th May 1998

Dear Kenzaburo,

I know so well your sense of helplessness before the banalisation of violence, the inability to feel the pain of others and the casual willingness to inflict it upon them, among which we are living. We are writers, not politicians, and as sometime political activists we are always among people better equipped for the role. Our writings are the 'essential gesture' (I quote Roland Barthes again, as I did for the title of one of my books) by which we reach out to grasp the hand of our society. But the vocation of literature seems so remote from violence; the hand we extend is struck aside by it. *Yet violence is also a means of expression.* That is what you and I have come to recognize. It is the way in which modern urban society *expresses* itself. If there is a means at all by which we can be effective, as writers, in striving to change this, it can only be to counter it by giving the alternative—in your words 'expression adequate enough to evoke imagination about death, violence and pain'.

'The imagination has been numbed.' You are right. Our task, laid heavily upon us by whatever talent we possess, is to attempt to bring it back to life. We are the bearers of that invisible chalk ring round the eye that the great Nigerian writer, Chinua Achebe, says marks the creative mind of those who know the power of the imagination to enrich existence. If violence is a means of expression, there is an alternative means of expression to satisfy that urgent human need. Therein is the common ground of what seems to be the tragic no-man's-land of the impoverished spirit, the wasteland between two irreconcilables, violence and the writer.

What then should we do, you ask? You raise on the eve of a new century a most chilling, foreboding aspect of mass media's manipulative distortion of the imagination, where it uses it at all.

You speak of the 'representation of chaotic future society . . . In images of a violent future world prevalent in the visual media are reflected . . . the society common to the present world.' In a word, the futuristic vision children and adults are being conditioned to is of a world where, expanded in space and continuing on earth, violence is normal, counter-violence is heroic. How do we go about bringing to our society awareness of the life-giving, life-enhancing alternative? Well, we have first to recognize the disagreeable fact that the grasp of mass media upon contemporary consciousness far exceeds our own engagement with it through serious literature. Writers, publishers, booksellers—our fraternity—cannot hope to challenge this head-on; what should be achievable is to *infiltrate* the media, in particular the aural and visual media. We shall have to lobby the culture ministries of our governments, the cultural administrators, the directors of TV and radio programmes, the advertisers whose money influences programme choices—all of these, to press for a phasing-out of the dominance of visual and aural pulp fiction and its replacement with the sight and sound of works that will revivify the capacities of the imagination in viewers/listeners who are stunned by the endless depiction of violence as an accepted means of expression in human relationships, whether between children or adults.

As novelists, you and I naturally think of the place of the novel in this context of imaginative literary forms. The novel is the most intellectually accessible to a general public, since it retains the advantage of the ancient roots of popular culture, story-telling. Would it be possible, you ask, for the novel to regain children and youths as its readers? And you make the important reservation: 'I am conceiving of the novel not as mere verbalisation of the visual media . . . I wish to regain the reader who will be reading this kind of novel with much wished-for intensity'.

It is true that the cultivation of imaginative power will not be attained by relying alone on introducing real literature in place of pulp fiction as the basis of television plays, or air-time, visual and oral, given to live readings instead of chat-shows. For a renaissance of the power of the imagination to bring the individual to re-examine his/her life, to restore the healing and humanising faculty of empathy—living beyond your own mind and flesh to feel with and identify with those of other people—we have to bring the individual back to the pleasures of what is written and printed between the covers of books. I emphasize 'pleasure' as what the reading of serious literature offers because 'serious' doesn't mean 'dull'. Humour is serious; playfulness is serious; satire is serious; all these are part of the means with which we equip ourselves to understand and deal with tragedy, love, anger, joy, disappointment, doubt. As novelists we have the whole range of human emotions and preoccupations in the abundance of the creative imagination. I am wary of any obligation to write 'down', to simplify these, as a supposed bait to attract children and youths. On the contrary, if we are both to infiltrate the media with literature and restore the unmatched experience of taking up a book and reading it *oneself*, we can do this only with integrity to the highest standards of our writing, the widest and deepest exploration of this life we share with our readers. We have to be equal to our aim of setting the imagination free through our own creative imagination, as great literature has always done, so that the reader, too, can visualize his/her own life beyond the bounds of publicity hype and the solution of violence.

To say goodbye, for the present; you hope for an encouraging word on the future, dear Kenzaburo. Am I a pessimist? A utopian? No; only a realistic optimist. So I'm putting together a modest book of some of the non-fiction pieces I've written, a reflection of how I've looked at this century I've lived in. The epigraph will reveal to you my conclusion of how it's been. The quote comes from a poem by our fellow Nobel laureate, Seamus Heaney:

> *History says,* don't hope
> On this side of the grave,
> *But then, once in a life-time*
> *The longed-for tidal wave*
> *Of justice can rise up,*
> *And hope and history rhyme.*

May we see history fulfil rather than betray our hopes for restoration of the power of the imagination in the new millennium.

Sincerely,
Nadine

How shall we look at each other then?

—Mongane Wally Serote

1959: WHAT IS APARTHEID?

M en are not born brothers; they have to discover each other, and it is this discovery that apartheid seeks to prevent.

What is apartheid?

It depends who's answering. If you ask a member of the South African government, he will tell you that it is separate and parallel development of white and black. If you ask an ordinary white man who supports the policy, he will tell you that it is the means of keeping South Africa white. If you ask a black man . . . well, he may give you any of a dozen answers arising out of whatever aspect of apartheid he has been brought up short against that day, for to him it is neither an ideological concept nor a policy, but a context in which his whole life, learning, working, loving, is rigidly enclosed. He could give you a list of the laws that restrict him from aspiring to most of the aims of any civilised person, or enjoying the pleasures that everyone else takes for granted. But it is unlikely that he will.

What may be on his mind at the moment is the problem of how to save his bright child from the watered down 'Bantu Education' which is now being substituted for standard education in schools for black children. Or perhaps you've merely caught him on the morning after he's spent a night in the police cells because he was out after curfew hours without a piece of paper bearing a white man's signature permitting him to do so. Perhaps (if he's a man who cares for such things) he's feeling resentful because there's a concert in town he'd not be permitted to attend, or (if he's the kind of man who isn't) he's irked at having to pay a black market price for a bottle of brandy he's debarred from buying legitimately. That's apartheid, to him.

All these things, big and little, and many more.

If you want to know how Africans—black men and women—live in South Africa, you will get in return for your curiosity an exposition of apartheid in action, for in all of a black man's life, all his life, rejection by the white man has the last word. With this word of rejection apartheid began, long before it hardened into laws and legislation, long before it became a theory of racial selectiveness and the policy of a government. The Afrikaner Nationalists did not invent it, they merely developed it, and the impulse of Cain from which they worked was and is present in many white South Africans, English-speaking as well as Afrikaner.

Shall I forget that when I was a child I was taught that I must never use a cup from which our servant had drunk?

I live in the white city of Johannesburg, the biggest city in South Africa. Around the white city, particularly to the west and north, is another city, black Johannesburg. This clear picture of black and white is blurred only a little at the edges by the presence of small Coloured (mixed blood) and Indian communities, also segregated, both from each other and the rest. You will see Africans in every house in the white city, of course, for every house has its servants' quarters, built not less than a certain minimum regulation distance from the white house. Sophisticated Africans call this backyard life 'living dogs-meat'—closer to the kennel and the outhouses than to the humans in the house. But no black man has his *home* in the white city; neither wealth nor honour or distinction of any kind could entitle him to move into a house in the street where I or any other white persons live. So it easily happens that thousands of white people live their whole lives without ever exchanging a word with a black man who is like themselves, on their own social and cultural level; and for them, the whole African people is composed of servants and the great army of "boys" who cart away or deliver things—the butcher's boy, the grocer's boy, the milk boy, the dust boy. On the basis of this experience, you will see that it is simple for white men and women to deduct that the black men and women are an inferior race. Out of this experience all the platitudes of apartheid sound endlessly, like the bogus sea from the convolutions of a big shell: *they're like children . . . they don't think the way we do . . . they're not ready . . .*

Black men do all the physical labour in our country, because no white man wants to dig a road or load a truck. But for every kind of work a white man *wants* to do, there are sanctions and job reservations to shut the black man out. In the building trade, and in industry, the Africans are the unskilled and semi-skilled workers, and they cannot, by law, become anything else. They cannot serve behind the counters in the shops, and cannot be employed alongside white clerks. Wherever they work, they cannot share the washrooms or the canteens of the white workers. But they may buy in the shops. Oh yes, once the

counter is between the black customer and the white shopkeeper, the hollow murmur of the apartheid shell is silenced—
they *are* ready, indeed, to provide a splendid market, they *do*
think enough like white people to want most of the things that
white people want, from LP recordings to no-iron shirts.

The real life of any community—restaurants, bars, hotels,
clubs, and coffee bars—has no place for the African man or
woman. They serve in all these, but they cannot come in and sit
down. Art galleries, cinemas, theatres, golf courses, and sports
clubs, even the libraries are closed to them. In the post offices
and all other government offices, they are served at segregated
counters.

What it means to live like this, from the day you are born
until the day you die, I cannot tell you. No white person can. I
think I know the lives of my African friends, but time and time
again I find that I have assumed, since it was so ordinary a part
of average experience, the knowledge in them of some commonplace experience that, in fact, they could never have had. How
am I to remember that Danny, who is writing his Ph.D. thesis
on industrial psychology, has never seen the inside of a
museum? How am I to remember that John, who is a journalist
on a lively newspaper, can never hope to see the film I am urg-
ing him not to miss, since the township cinemas are doubly
censored and do not show what one might call adult films?
How am I to remember that Alice's charming children, playing
with my child's toy elephant, will never be able to ride on the
elephant in the Johannesburg Zoo?

The humblest labourer will find his life the meaner for being
black. If he were a white man, at least there would be no ceiling
to his children's ambitions. But it is in the educated man that
want and need stand highest on the wrong side of the colour
bar. Whatever he achieves as a man of learning, *as a man* he still

has as little say in the community as a child or a lunatic. Outside the gates of the university (soon he may not be able to enter them at all; the two 'open' universities are threatened by legislation that will close them to all who are not white) white men will hail him as 'boy'. When the first African advocate was called to the Johannesburg Bar, just over a year ago, government officials raised objections to his robing and disrobing in the same chamber as the white advocates. His colleagues accepted him as a man of the law; but the laws of apartheid saw him only as a black man. Neither by genius nor cunning, by sainthood or thuggery, is there a way in which a black man can earn the right to be regarded as any other man.

Of course, the Africans have made some sort of life of their own. It's a slum life, a make-do life, because, although I speak of black cities outside white cities, these black cities are no Harlems. They are bleak rectangular patterns of glum municipal housing, or great smoky proliferations of crazy, chipped brick and tin huts, with a few street-lights and few shops. The life there is robust, ribald, and candid. All human exchange of the extrovert sort flourishes; standing in a wretched alley, you feel the exciting blast of a great vitality. Here and there, in small rooms where a candle makes big shadows, there is good talk. It is attractive, specially if you are white; but it is also sad, bleak, and terrible. It may not be a bad thing to be a Sophiatown Villon; but it is tragic if you can never be anything else. The penny whistle is a charming piece of musical ingenuity; but it should not always be necessary for a man to make his music out of nothing.

Some Africans are born, into their segregated townships, light enough to pass as Coloured. They play Coloured for the few privileges—better jobs, better housing, more freedom of movement—that this brings, for the nearer you can get to being white, the less restricted your life is. Some Coloureds are born, into their segregated townships, light enough to pass as white. A fair skin is the equivalent of a golden spoon in the child's mouth; in other countries coloured people may be tempted to play white for social reasons, but in South Africa a pale face and straight hair can gain the basic things—a good school, acceptance instead of rejection all the way along the line. It is the ambition of many coloured parents to have a child light enough to cross the colour bar and live the precarious life of pretending to be white; their only fear is that the subterfuge will be discovered. But, the other night, I was made aware of a different sort of fear and a new twist to the old game of play-white. An Indian acquaintance confessed to me that he was uneasy because his thirteen-year-old son has turned out to have the sort of face and complexion that could pass for white. 'He's only got to slip into a white cinema or somewhere, just once, for the fun of it. The next thing my wife and I know he'll be starting to play white. Once they've tried what it's like to be a white man, how are you to stop them? Then it's the lies, and not wanting to know their own families, and misery all round. That's one of the reasons why I want to leave South Africa, so's my kids won't want to grow up to be something they're not.'

I've talked about the wrong side of the colour bar, but the truth is that both are the wrong sides. Do not think that we, on the white side of privilege, are the people we might be in a society that had no sides at all. We do not suffer, but we are coarsened. Even to continue to live here is to acquiesce in some measure to apartheid—to a sealing-off of responses, the cauterisation of the human heart, as well as to withholding the vote from those who outnumber us, eight to one. Our children grow up accepting as part of natural phenomena the fact that they are well-clothed and well-fed, while black children are ragged and skinny. It cannot occur to the white child that the black one has any rights outside of charity; you must explain to your child, if you have the mind to, that men have decided this, that the white shall have, and the black shall have not, and it is not an immutable law, like the rising of the sun in the morning. Even then it is not possible entirely to counter with facts an emotional climate of privilege. We have the better part of everything; how difficult it is for us not to feel, somewhere secretly, that we *are* better?

Hundreds of thousands of white South Africans are concerned only with holding on to white privilege. They believe that they would rather die holding on to it than give up the smallest part; and I believe they would. They cannot imagine a life that would be neither their life, nor the black man's life, but another life altogether. How can they imagine freedom, who for years have had to be so vigilant to keep it only to themselves?

No one of us, black or white, can promise them that black domination will not be the alternative to white domination, and black revenge the long if not the last answer to all that the whites have done to the blacks. For such is apartheid that, like many whites, many blacks cannot imagine a life that would be neither a black man's life or a white man's life.

Those white South Africans who want to let go—leave hold—are either afraid of having held on too long, or are disgusted and ashamed to go on living as we do. These last have become colour-blind, perhaps by one of those freaks by which desperate nature hits upon a new species. They want another life altogether, in South Africa. They want people of all colours to use the same doors, share the same learning, and give and take the same respect from each other. They don't care if the government that guarantees these things is white or black. A few of these people go so far as to go to prison, in the name of one political cause or another, in attempts that they believe will help to bring about this sort of life. The rest make, in one degree or another, an effort to live, within an apartheid community, the decent life that apartheid prohibits.

Of course, I know that no African attaches much importance to what apartheid does to the white man, and no-one could blame him for this. What does it signify that your sense of justice is outraged, your conscience troubled, and your friendships restricted by the colour bar? All very commendable that your finer feelings are affronted—he's the one who gets it in the solar plexus. All this lies heavily, mostly unspoken, between black and white friends. My own friends among black men and women are people I happen to like, my kind of people, whose friendship I am not prepared to forego because of some racial theory that I find meaningless and absurd. Like that of many others, my opposition to apartheid is compounded not only out of a sense of justice, but also out of a personal, selfish, and extreme distaste for having the choice of my friends dictated to me, and the range of human intercourse proscribed for me. I am aware that, because of this, I sometimes expect African friends to take lightly, in the ordinary course of friendship, risks that simply are not worth it, to them, who have so many more basic things to risk themselves for. I remember a day last year when some African friends and I went to the airport to see off a close friend of us all. I had brought a picnic lunch with me, and so had Alice, my friend, for we knew that we shouldn't be able to lunch together in the airport restaurant. What we hadn't realised was that we shouldn't be allowed to sit outside on the grass together and eat, either; "non-Europeans" were not supposed to be admitted to the lawns. I wanted to brazen it out, sit there until we were ordered off into segregation; it was easy for me, I am white and not sensitised by daily humiliations. But Alice, who has to find words to explain to her children why they cannot ride the elephant at the zoo, did not want to seek the sort of rebuff that comes to her all the time, unsought.

Black and white get to know each other in spite of and under the strain of a dozen illegalities. We can never meet in town, for there is nowhere we can sit and talk together. The legal position about receiving African guests in a white house is unclear; we do have our friends in our houses, of course, but there is always the risk that a neighbour may trump up a complaint, to which the police would always be sympathetic. When you offer an African guest a drink, you break the law unequivocally; the exchange of a glass of beer between your hands and his could land you both in the police court on a serious charge. Officially, you are not supposed to enter an African 'location' without a permit, and when we go to visit friends in a black township we take the chance of being stopped by the police, who are looking for gangsters or caches of liquor, but will do their duty to apartheid on the side. Three days ago I was one of a small group of whites who had to get up and leave the table at the wedding reception of an African medical student; a white official of the gold-mining company for whom the bride's father worked, and on whose property his house was, drove up to inform us that our invitations to the wedding were not sufficient to authorise our presence in living quarters provided for Africans.

No friendship between black and white is free of these things. It is hard to keep any relationship both clandestine and natural. No matter how warm the pleasure in each other's company, how deep and comfortable the understanding, there are moments of failure created by resentment of white privilege, on the one side, and guilt about white privilege on the other.

Another life altogether.

Put the shell to your ear and hear the old warning: Do you want to be overrun by blacks?

I bump an African's scooter while parking, and before he and I have a chance to apologise or accuse, there's a white man at my side ready to swear that I'm in the right, and there are three black men at his side ready to swear that he is in the right.

Another life altogether.

Put the shell to your ear and hear the old warning: Are you prepared to see white standards destroyed?

A friend of mine, a dignified and responsible African politician and an old man, is beaten up by white intruders while addressing a meeting of dignified and responsible white people.

Living apart, black and white are destroying themselves morally in the effort. Living together, it is just possible that we might survive white domination, black domination, and all the other guises that hide us from each other, and discover ourselves to be identically human. The least we could all count on would be the recognition that we have no more and no less reason to fear each other than other men have.

—*Africa Seminar*
Washington, D.C., 1959

HOW NOT TO KNOW

THE AFRICAN

———◦◦◦◦———

A few months ago, 1st April 1966—April Fool's Day—
I read in a Johannesburg newspaper an advertisement
for a course of lectures entitled *Know the African*. From
the description given, it was clear that these lectures were
designed for white people who have the only recognised relationship with coloured people in our country—that of white
employer to black labour force—and who might find it useful,
from the point of view of efficiency, to get to know just enough
human facts about these units of labour to get them to give of
their best. This sort of study of 'the African' as a strange creature whom one must know how to 'handle' in the eight hours
he spends at work is apparently the limit of getting to 'know
the African' permissible to South Africans, nowadays. For that
same week there appeared in the papers an announcement of the
ban, under the 1965 Suppression of Communism Amendment
Act, on the utterances and writings of forty-six South Africans
living abroad, and this list included *all* those black South

African writers of any note not already silenced by other bans. The work of our country's African and Coloured prose writers is now non-existent, so far as South African literature, South African thinking, South African culture, is concerned. They were the voices—some rasping, some shrill, some clowning, some echoing prophetically, one or two deeply analytical—of the thirteen millions on the other side of the colour bar. We shall not hear from them again.

White people are likely to come back pat as Pretty Polly with the remark that these African and Coloured writers who have been banned, gagged, and censored are, after all, a handful of intellectuals, completely unrepresentative of the ordinary people in the streets, locations, and kraals. What could one hear from them but the inevitable dissatisfaction of all intellectuals, exacerbated by the fact that they are black?

Of all the self-delusion white South Africans practise, this is perhaps the purest example. Who, of any group, in any society, formulates the aspirations, makes coherent the inchoate resentments, speaks the dreams of the mass of people who cannot express these things for themselves? Who, anywhere in the world, translates the raw material of the human condition, which millions experience but for which millions have no words? Would the private history—lived in the minds of all Afrikaners, whatever their station—of the Afrikaner's bitternesses, hopes, and joys, the shaping of his attitudes in relation to circumstances over three hundred years, have been recorded if this had been left to the nation's stokers and mine shiftbosses? The Afrikaners' writers and poets spoke for them—their handful of intellectuals. The same applies to English-speaking white South Africans; their handful of intellectuals and writers are the medium through which the currents of their thought see the light as communication.

The silenced African and Coloured writers are, indeed, nothing but a handful among millions of ordinary labourers and domestic servants; and in their work they express what all these people could never, would never, say.

If we want to know—not 'the African', that laboratory specimen, that worker bee of fascinating habits, but the black men and women amongst whom we live, these writers are the only people from whom we could learn. They are not pedagogues or politicians; with the exception of the former Cape Town councillor, Alex La Guma, and Dennis Brutus and Alfred Hutchinson, none of them has ever been accused of involvement in practical politics. When they do deal with politics in their writings, they are short on political abstraction and long on personal anecdote. Some are not 'serious' at all, and the self-parody is as revealing as the Jewish joke (I am thinking of Todd Matshikiza's zany and delightful autobiography, *Chocolates for My Wife*). Some exaggerate wildly a life whose everyday degradation and brutality, under our eyes in the faces of the dagga-smoking children thieving about Johannesburg streets—those "picannins" who are a feature of our way of life—would hardly seem to need it, and the exaggeration in itself becomes a revelation of the posturing fantasy bred by such a life. (I am thinking of Bloke Modisane's *Blame Me on History*.) All of them, from Can Themba writing his few short stories in an overblown yet pungent prose dipped in the potent brew of back-street urban life, to Ezekiel Mphahlele writing with dry lucidity (*Down Second Avenue*) of childhood in one of those mud huts you pass on the road, near Pietersburg, offer a firsthand account of the life that is lived out of sight of the white suburbs, and the thoughts that lie unspoken behind dark faces. If one wants to know more than a few poor facts, these autobiographies, novels, stories, essays, and poems are the place to find the inner world where men learn the things worth knowing about each other.

Many of these works are what I call 'escape' books: the record either of the fear and hazard of an actual physical escape from South Africa without passport or permit, or the other kind of escape, less finally and sometimes never accomplished—the slow escape, within the writer's self, from the apartheid cara-pace of second-class citizen, and the retrospective bitterness that threatens to poison life, once outside it. Ezekiel Mphahlele's autobiographical *Down Second Avenue*, Matshikiza's *Chocolates for My Wife*, Hutchinson's *Road to Ghana*—escape books all, in their different ways—entered South Africa after publication in England, and were on sale here for a time before being banned. One of the first and perhaps the most movingly artless 'escape' book, *Tell Freedom*, by Peter Abrahams, was banned, although it had been out of print for years and the writer was long in exile. Modisane's *Blame Me on History* and Mphahlele's next book, *African Images*, a collection of essays, were banned before they reached the bookshops, and Alex La Guma's novel and the poems of Dennis Brutus were automati-cally withheld because both writers were under personal bans. Dennis Brutus's little volume of poetry consists mainly of love lyrics; Alex La Guma's *A Walk in the Night* is, so far as I am aware, the only novel to come out of District Six—a slum story notable for a curiously impressive, fastidious, obsessive horror at the touch, taste, and smell of poverty.

These writers—with the exception of Abrahams and Hutchinson, whose books are banned individually—are under total ban now, and we cannot read what they have written, nor shall we be able to read what they may write in the future. One whose name I have not mentioned yet, Lewis Nkosi, is probably the greatest loss to us of them all. This young man, who left his home in South Africa on an exit permit in 1965, published a book of essays entitled *Home and Exile*. I took the opportunity to buy and read the essays while on a visit to Zambia, for Lewis

Nkosi is on the list of exiles whose word and work are under that blanket ban of April this year. The book contains critical writing of a standard that has never before been achieved by a South African writer, white or black. Here is the sibling Edmund Wilson, Lionel Trilling, F. R. Leavis we have never had. If the ban on his work did not prevent me quoting from two of the essays—the first a brilliant exploration of the conflict between truth as the individual has laboured to discover it for himself and truth as the glib public proposition dictated by the contingencies of political life; the second a cool, erudite look at fiction written by black South Africans—it would not be necessary for anyone to take my word for it. The book is divided into three sections. 'Home' includes an autobiographical chronicle of the fifties in Johannesburg that might perhaps have been entitled 'Know the White Man', had Nkosi with his wit and candour not long since outgrown the categorical approach. 'Exile' contains two fascinating encounters with New York that ring with the overwrought sensibility of the stranger in town. 'Literary', the outstanding section, is devoted to criticism of life and letters. The book clearly does not seek to present final answers on the author's behalf, but deals with questions proposed to him by exile and the perspective of foreign countries. It is a long hard look at South Africa, at himself, at all of us, black and white, among whom he belongs.

In 1963 I wrote about the proliferating forms of restriction of free expression in our country, in general, and the effect of the (then) new Publications and Entertainments Act in particular. I pointed out that most of the writings of black South Africans who had recorded the contemporary experience of their people were banned; the process is now completed. No association of writers or intellectuals, English or Afrikaans, has protested against this virtual extinction of black and Coloured

South African writers. One can only repeat, with a greater sense of urgency, the questions I asked then: These books were written in English and they provide the major part of the only record, set down by talented and self-analytical people, of what black South Africans, who have no voice in parliament or any say in the ordering of their life, think and feel about their lives and those of their fellow white South Africans. Can South Africa afford to do without these books?

And can South Africans boast of a 'literature' while, by decree, in their own country, it consists of *some* of the books written by its black and white, Afrikaans and English-speaking writers?

—1966

A MORNING IN
THE LIBRARY: 1975

———❧—–—

Recently I spent a strange morning in a library.

It was the Reference Section of the Johannesburg Municipal Library; I had entered, made my request to a solicitously-attentive librarian, followed her to a glass-fronted case, waited while she unlocked it and removed a large, loose-leafed volume for me.

Now I sat down with the other users of the library at one of the drawing-room-glossy tables. It was good to find myself among people of all colours, absorbed in their reading; faded and ridiculous, those days not long ago, when to work here and take advantage of the courteous and knowledgeable help of the librarians whites kept for themselves. A crumbling at the edges of the apartheid fortress had at least taken place. Now all my fellow Johannesburgers were surrounded by books. Some had piled a lair against distraction; some stared at an array set out like a hand of patience. A young girl opposite me was making notes, hovering from source to source above spread volumes. Quietly, with the creaking of boots or the lisp of crêpe rubber, the offices of this temple of learning were performed as people went back and forth between the shelves, taking and replacing books, more books.

I alone had only one before me. It occupied me the whole morning; it was, in a sense, the Book of Books, whose word is set up against that of all others. My book was *Jacobsen's Index of Objectionable Literature,* the bible of South African censorship. And so, while the search for knowledge, know-how, spiritual enlightenment, and the pleasures of poetry went on about me— like most writers, I am as practised a squinter as I am an eaves-dropper, and I noted Wittgenstein, *Teach Yourself Accountancy, Pascal's Pensées, Seventeenth Century English Verse*—I read on down the lists of banned books in *Jacobsen.*

There is a great deal of trash, of course. Paperbacks of the kind that are twirled round on wire stands in chewing-gum-and-smokes shops and airports; the titles of the banned ones don't sound any different from those I see on sale everywhere. The sheer volume of sub-literature swamps the resources of censorship, in that category. And there are books I suppose we could be said to be lucky to do without? Dr Rubin never gets a chance to tell us Everything We Always Wanted to Know About Sex and Were Afraid to Ask.

The 'highest literary judgment' South Africans are con-stantly assured is a qualification of the government-appointed censors who consider literature, plays, and films apparently is just as good for extra-literary purposes: the censors are expected to bring this judgment to bear upon and indeed have banned T-shirts bearing saucy legends, a black fist, and even the peace sign. Let us not bother to recall the famous panty-hose packet; there was also a glass that, on being filled with liquid, showed the figure of a nude woman. There they are, listed in *Jacobsen*.

But it's easy to laugh at the South African censors. Our amusement, their solemn ridiculousness—these have not undermined their power. Indeed, as we know, the renewed and tightened censorship legislation (it was first imposed in the sixties) that came into force on April 1 this year protects the newly-chosen personnel both from ridicule and from exposure should their decisions be challenged. The right of appeal to a court of law against bannings has been taken from writers, and it is now an offence against the law to criticise members of the special Appeal Board set up within the censorship organization to hear appeals against decisions made by its own regional censorship committees.

Most titles my finger was running down, page after page, were banned by the old Publications Control Board, before April. They constitute virtually the entire *oeuvre* of black South African fiction writers, essayists, and some poets, including Lewis Nkosi, Alex La Guma, Ezekiel Mphahlele and Dennis Brutus, and individual works by myself, Jack Cope, Mary Benson, C. J. Driver, André Brink, and others, black and white.

Bans on British, American, and European writers include works by Kingsley Amis, Vladimir Nabokov, Bernard Malamud, Norman Mailer, John O'Hara, John Masters, James Baldwin, Edna O'Brien, John Updike, Frederic Raphael, Joseph Heller, Robert Penn Warren, Gore Vidal, Han Suyin, James Purdy, William Burroughs, Erica Jong, Langston Hughes, Doris Lessing, Paul Theroux, Truman Capote, Alan Sillitoe, Sinclair Lewis, William Styron, Alison Lurie, Phillip Roth, Jakov Lind, J. P. Donleavy, Kurt Vonnegut, and Jack Kerouac. Translations include books by Joseph Kessel, Jean-Paul Sartre, Romain Gary, Alberto Moravia, Carlos Fuentes, Roger Peyrefitte, Jean Genet, Francoise Mallet-Joris, Junichiro Tanazaki, Alain Robbe-Grillet, Colette, Nikos Kazantzakis, Jean Cocteau, Alfred Jarry, Vasco Pratolini, Vladimir Mayakovsky, Marguerite Duras, Guy de Maupassant, and Pierre Louÿs.

Among contemporary thinkers there are works by Herbert Marcuse, Oscar Lewis, Salvador Allende, Wilhelm Reich, Louis Althusser, and Leszek Kolakowski.

Some of the bannings of the new censorship organization were too recent yet to have found their place in *Jacobsen's Index*. Iris Murdoch's *The Black Prince* was one. Wopko Jensma's *Where White Is the Colour, Black Is the Number*, Mary Benson's *The Sun Will Rise*, and Breyten Breytenbach's latest work, were others. And the day after I spent my morning in the library reading about what we may not read, our new and greatly enlarged team of censors showed nothing if not extraordinary breadth of literary judgment—at one eclectic stroke they banned George Lukács's *History and Class Consciousness* and thirteen pairs of men's underpants bearing legends such as 'Long John Silver'.

If you don't believe me, you can go to our library and look it all up in the Book of Books.

HEROES AND VILLAINS

Pascale, my French granddaughter, aged four and enraged at not getting her own way, would shriek at her mother, '*Vilaine!*' It seems to me there's something both childish and archaic about the word 'villain', although the English epithet has a harsher meaning. More or less dropped out of common usage, it belongs to vanished melodrama and has somehow reverted to that definition listed in the OED as 'now rare': someone boorish, clownish rather than evil. But if I am to accept the word as current coinage for an evil person, I'm not sure I know any villains personally. And we all know that so far as public figures are concerned, one individual's villain is the next one's hero. Many of us live or have lived under regimes whose morality has never been described better than by Chinua Achebe in his novel *A Man of the People*: 'Overnight, everyone began to shake their heads at the excesses of the last regime, at its graft, oppression and corrupt government . . . everybody said

what a terrible lot; and it became public opinion next morning.
And these were the same people that only the other day owned
a thousand names of adulation, whom praise-singers followed
with song and talking drum wherever they went. In such a
regime, I say, you died a good death if your life had inspired
someone to come forward and shoot your murderers in the
chest—without asking to be paid.'

Substitute the front page and CNN for those societies lack-
ing song and talking drums, and you have a description of wide
and timely application, eh.

In a novel I wrote in the seventies I had one of my characters
remark that it was strange to live in a country where there were
still heroes. Her country was mine, and this is something I, too,
am aware of. To sit out more than two decades as a prisoner of
conscience, as my heroes Mandela, Sisulu, and others whose
names wouldn't mean anything to you, have done, and come
out whole, sane, wise, and humorous, is unambiguously heroic.
To endure the amputation of exile is heroic; I see that in men
and women who are returning home to South Africa now.

I have known some of these heroes quite well; a wonderful
and salutary experience I count as one of the most important
even among the intimacies of my life. This is because such people cut one to size in terms of one's own worth and yet assert with
authority, in their very existence, that life is passionately worth
living. Is this where heroism and villainy meet, in the electri-
cally-charged field of avid energy? We look on from the outside,
aghast in the one instance, admiring in the other. The persistence of evil appalling, the endurance of good awe-inspiring.

But some heroes present a categorical enigma. They started
off in the ranks of evil, so far as the judgment of people who
reject any practice of racism is concerned, and then they
rebelled against and rejected the convictions of those ranks.

This was not an easy matter of making statements, resigning from some political formation; often it meant losing professional position, livelihood, and being prepared to face a probation of suspicion in the ranks of opposition to racism.

In a house not far from mine there is one of my heroes who lived for some years as, in my apartheid code, a villain. Dr. Beyers Naudé is an Afrikaner who was brought up in the era when the National Party was still avenging the defeat of the Boer War and seeking through that pious villainy, nationalism claiming authority from religion, to restore its dignity by coming to power. He became a minister in the Dutch Reformed Church and a member of the *Broederbond*, the band of brothers, a secret society of ideological guerrillas who dominated successive apartheid governments under prime ministers who were their Broeders. When he was a young man with a wife and children he committed the heresy of declaring apartheid sinful and he was stripped of his ministry; he rejected the *Broederbond* and consequently was blackballed from any secular position in Afrikanerdom.

He looked, and still looks, like the prototype Afrikaner *dominee*, wearing the Afrikaner outfit of safari suit, with plastered-down hair above his earnestly smiling face. But out of this (believe me) endearing image—which somehow subconsciously demonstrates his belief that within the conventional Afrikaners he resembles outwardly there is light like his own waiting to be self-realized—has come amazing courage. He was banned, vilified, and harassed by apartheid governments. He had no ministry, but we were all, all of us in the struggle against racism, his congregation. The enormous risks he has taken to support black liberation can't yet be fully told, because that liberation is not by any means fully achieved, but to the black liberation movement he has become the most trusted white individual in South Africa.

How is it that 'villain' and 'hero' have existed in one man in one lifetime? He would put his conversion down to God, I know. But as I have no god, I am still looking for an explanation. Conscience? Isn't that an atavistic conditioning that comes from the *thou shalts* and *thou shalt nots*, even in unbelievers? Sense of justice, that spirit-level indicator, origin unknown?

—1991

CRACK THE NUT:

THE FUTURE BETWEEN

YOUR TEETH

<hr />

It is usual in a graduation address to tell the graduates how they ought to live. But I can't tell you that. My own generation has not been able to make of our country a sane society aiming for social justice. After a foreign war in which white and black South Africans died to defeat world domination based on racism, the survivors came back and with those who had stayed behind created systematically, out of the same blood-prejudices they had fought, the ideology and practice of apartheid. Some of our thinkers, graduates of South African universities, claim for this most primitive and atavistic social theory that it is so boldly progressive it can't be grasped by those whose nineteenth-century liberalism, born of the principles of 1789, it outdates; and that its white theologically-endorsed justice is beyond any that could be envisaged by the materialist concepts of the Left. Those who opposed apartheid have been, in the case of whites, too few to prevail; with highly courageous exceptions, many of whom ended in jail, exile, or remain among us silenced under bans, they have been opponents weak in conviction, strong on caution. In the case of blacks, their numerical superiority and moral force—the right of the wronged and oppressed that ploughs down palaces and towers—have not been able to prevail against arms dug in behind an implacably discriminating economy.

This university has, in the foyer of the Great Hall in which we are gathered, a plaque which avows:

At a general assembly of the university held on the 16th April, 1959 the following dedication was affirmed:

We are gathered here today to affirm in the name of the University of the Witwatersrand that it is our duty

To uphold the principle that a university is a place where men and women without regard to race or colour are welcome to join in the acquisition and advancement of knowledge.

And to continue faithfully to defend this ideal against all who have sought by legislative enactment to curtail the autonomy of the University.

Now therefore we dedicate ourselves to the maintenance of this ideal and to the restoration of the autonomy of our university.

That plaque was put in place twenty-one years ago, but its dedication has not been fulfilled. It has not been fulfilled despite the efforts of a series of just and enlightened chancellors and principals, a student body that with each successive intake has included young men and women who have worked through the Students' Representative Council to that end, and thousands of graduates, some of whom have become prominent citi-

zens, who should not have lost sight of it in the influential positions they hold in South African society. I cannot tell you to
cherish what we have; I can only turn around the proposition
and ask you to try to create something worth cherishing.

To attempt this it seems to me you will first have to come to
a clear and honest understanding of your position. I use the
word 'position' in the singular, although there are some black
graduates at Wits (about ten percent of the student body represents the hard-won progress made since the plaque was set up)
and although the situations of black and white are totally different, because both black and white do inherit in common a
state of underdevelopment of a specific kind. We have the most
highly-industrialized state in Africa, we have gold, diamonds,
uranium, coal, etc., a technology and achievements in science
and medicine second to none on this continent and in many
countries beyond, but we are also in the state of underdevelopment defined by the Cuban novelist Edmundo Desnoes and
described of his own country as an inability to relate things, to
accumulate experience meaningfully. What happened to South
Africa after the Second World War is the most obvious example. But experience is an accretion of day-to-day life rather than
the sum of large events. It is the failure to relate that experience
to historical change, on the one hand, and to a fixed and unalterable sense of the rights of human existence, on the other, that
is symptomatic of this kind of underdevelopment.

Now, what do I mean by historical change, vis-à-vis your life?

I mean quite simply and unequivocally that you have been
brought up on the white side or the black side of whatever
so-called community you have been born to; you have gone to a
segregated school during your most malleable years; you have
unthinkingly, as we all have, climbed on buses and entered cinemas and numerous other public places reserved for people of

your skin-color—able as they are to go anywhere, whites, certainly, even the most aware, cannot be conscious twenty-four hours a day of the bizarre and unnatural character of what is commonplace in their lives, and even blacks, chafed into greater awareness by the restrictions that debar them everywhere, and perhaps even more by the patronising concessions that now allow them into the public library in this town but not in that, seat them beside a white on South African Airways but not on trains and buses, must often take these circumstances for granted. Yet from these daily acceptances comes the sense of self, of one's place in the world, of a recognized identity; and in your case, a very peculiar one, as consciously conditioned as if you were to have been born into one of those science fiction worlds where people are cloned to function as drones, soldiers, or breeders. This historical identity that my generation has handed on to you is a thing of the past; an immature image of self, a contradiction of your humanity; useless to you; an encumbrance to be consciously shed.

What do I mean by a fixed and unalterable sense of the rights of human existence? Don't these change from country to country and ideology to ideology? And don't all countries and ideologies claim sole guardianship of them?

But I am talking of something comparable only to the middle ear in the human head, an aural organ but also the seat of balance, by which we find our way upright; I don't know where the seat of a fixed and unalterable sense of the rights of human existence lies, and how many millennia of successive descents into and emergings from barbarism have gone to establish it through how many media, instinctive, mythical, religious, philosophical—but I am convinced this sense does exist between the fire and ice, the dreadful polar caps of human behavior. It is not a mystery, it's a balance. We know what we are; we know what we might be. At the axis of the propositions is the sense of the rights of human existence, and that sense is never quite lost, as evidenced in the elaborate justification for its distortion, propped up by Hansard volumes, Commission reports, by rhetoric, bombast, and propaganda of all kinds and from all sides. The sense of the rights of human existence is there inside you, like your unseen middle ear—a collective conscience painfully arrived at, characteristic of your humankind, if you prefer. And it is to this sense—the true *sense*, your own sanity—that your daily accumulation of experience needs to be measured and related, and not to the shifty accommodations of a dying experiment called separate development and about to be renamed a 'constellation of states'.

If you are going to graduate only by means of your degree, you may count yourself well-educated but I do not think you will be fully equipped to live your life in South Africa now. A few years ago I was on a television programme in the United States, and the black South African actor Winston Ntshona, also taking part, was asked by the interviewer: 'What advice would you give Nadine Gordimer as a white South African?'

Ntshona thought for a moment and said, 'I'd tell her, live like a man.'

The interviewer got his laugh even if he hadn't managed to draw blood as he'd no doubt hoped. But I didn't laugh and Ntshona didn't laugh. We understood each other; I knew what he meant, and so do you. Without any apologies to my sisters in this gathering, I am conscious of how far I have failed to 'live like a man'. To attempt to be fully human in South Africa it is necessary to examine your actions and their consequences, to view your private experience in relation not only to the section of society, the enclave in which it has been accumulating, but in relation to the complexity of the society as a whole in which you live; to see your existence not only in relation to nuclear family, friends, economic, professional, and social group, but to the human matrix in which these, and you, are embedded. That is where you are—not, as apartheid has made it seem, safe in your commune on an old mining property, in chambers where you receive your clients, the consulting rooms and wards where you examine your patients, the speech clinics and social welfare offices where you help people overcome their personal problems, the disco where only the lights change, the country club or suburban garden where everything seems to stay the same.

As you leave this university, you need to look back and think about what your presence here for a number of years has signified. Everyone will tell you you have been privileged. This is a platitude taken over unquestioningly from other societies where class, a flexible concept, or exceptional ability, arguably a determinant of congenital and/or environmental origin, is the criterion. The implication is that you are privileged because higher education will put up your worth in the market-place and/or qualify you to serve the community at a high level of skill; and the intellectual stimulation you have received will bloom as your capacity for living fully. But in South Africa the concept of 'privilege' has acquired stronger negative than positive associations. The privilege of a good education is not one that can be earned by exceptional ability, hard work, or even parents' will to pay for it. You have first to be born white; and if you are, you have to remain aware that this 'privilege' from which so many others are spawned is also a mark of Cain; while some are embracing you in congratulation, others are cursing you. If you are white, that is your sober heritage. That is the truth of your situation on this day.

If you are a black graduate, you have to be aware that you have been made an exception of rather than given the right to the same education for black South Africans as for white. That is the truth of your situation on this day.

I cannot tell you—all of you, black and white—you have nothing to fear from the truth. There is plenty to fear in South Africa; but it is no pious platitude to say that the greatest danger lies in not seeing facts, not admitting them, walking out of here in your new-found, qualified adulthood to take up life *the way it is*. Because life *the way it is* in South Africa is over. Young blacks don't need telling; indeed, they are the ones who are spelling out, thinking out, acting out the message. The old laws are still there, the old forms are still there, but the laws are hollow and the men and women are not. They are purposeful and mutually support-ive, eager to prepare themselves for the future. It is for young white men and women that I want to put up a banner over the exits of the Great Hall, near the plaque: Don't walk out of this university into the past. You will not be going into the old fam-ily business that grew from slavery to apartheid. Free yourself gladly of the mentality that went with that kind of enterprise.

Despite the questionable nature of privilege in our country, I think there *has* been a certain element of unquestionable privi-lege about your years at Wits, and I rejoice in it for all of you, black and white. This is a segregated university, it has only a token if growing presence of black students, and while race laws remain this cannot be otherwise; and I know that repeating the die-stamp of the immediate world outside the campus, student life tends to equate like-seeking-like with pigment seeking like pigment—so that there are clubs and groups who see their interests as defensively racially-defined. In present circum-stances in South Africa this is not surprising. Under apartheid, the fact that you are African black or Indian black or Chinese or white is the most important characteristic you have. The full preposterousness of this morbid phenomenon will be booming our shame loud-mouthed through ages when all else about life *the way it is* among us has long been forgotten.

But in spite of all this, you have lived a less absurd and corrupting life for the hours you have spent on this campus every day than is lived outside it. I hope for your own sakes the difference has marked you deeply. I hope you will never disavow it; I hope you won't cover it with some sleazy, fashionable life-style; I hope even more that you will not regard it as a campaign medal to be trotted out for the rest of your life in lieu of any further thought and action—that there won't come from any of you that vapid death-rattle: Oh, when I was a student I used to get steamed up about things—

At this university you have had the chance to be stirred and informed, to wake up and muster the momentum of doubts, questionings, polemical argument in public in a way that is not possible outside these gates. For study purposes at least you have had access to works expressing ideas—the movement of modern thought, the expression of changing concepts of man in his sexual, political, religious, and social being—that are banned from libraries and bookshops outside. You have been able at least to take a breath in an atmosphere where, in some intellectual disciplines, a new concept of South African culture is being explored—as, for example, in Professor John Dugard's Applied Legal Studies; in work being done in the fields of social science, psychology, and film; in T. J. Couzens' establishment in our literature of the journalism and other writings by early black writers, and Professor Charles van Onselen's social history of this extraordinary area in which we live—the Witwatersrand—as an analytic assertion of values of other than the gold price.

These are the inklings of a new idea of yourself to be realized in relation not to the inherited illusions strung around your neck but to the real entities of the life that has always been there, about you; the understanding that an exclusively white-based culture has been and is as foreign and sterile for white South Africans as for black, and that there is a huge new cultural energy ready to blow—our popular hero-figure doesn't have to be Kojak, and our humour isn't really Carol Burnett's.

Here at this university you have had a chance to learn how you have been manipulated by the forces of a particular social order, and the more general social forces in conflict in the world. You have come to question, many of you, the politics, economics, and mores of home and class as well as colour, that you were born to, outside the university. You have had a chance to make contact as equals, however tenuously, across the colour taboos maintained by harsh penalty outside. If you have not made use of these opportunities to remake yourself, the loss is yours, the lack is yours. If you have made use of them, you have gained a foothold in independence of mind from which arbitrary doctrines will find it difficult to coax you down, and ministerial demagogues to cow you.

In 1971, when I gave the Academic Freedom Lecture at the University of Natal, I remarked that the places of public assembly in South Africa were by then open only to dog shows and pop groups. In 1980 this has not changed—except to get worse, since there were to be further restrictions after 1976 and these have just been renewed. Because you were a student at this university, last month you were able to be present at a public meeting that could not take place in a public square, and you heard the free and fearless expression of ideas about the state of your country, the future of your country, that would be most unlikely to be given a platform outside the environment of a university. And because you were there, openly expressing your solidarity on an issue openly stated, you know that it is not true that your signature on an appeal to free Nelson Mandela is an approval of urban terrorism. You know that your signature among more than fifty thousand others was consciously and responsibly an action to create a real alternative to the horrors of terrorism. Unlike hundreds of thousands of other South Africans who only get the chance to hear what the government wants them to hear, you will know that what the Minister of Police has implied of your action is not the truth. And that is important. A single meeting; a single issue; but with significance for your whole life to come, where you will again and again be faced with the need to examine your facts and hold your convictions on that evidence alone, against pervasive and persuasive interpretations that others will try to sell you, if not to brand you with.

Take all these advantages away with you from the university, along with your professional skill; use them, develop them along with it. Graduation from the peculiarly South African state of underdevelopment has not been accomplished as your degree has been granted, once and for all. People will taunt you fearfully— you yourself will not be without fear—how do you know, if you must abandon South Africa the way it is, the way it will be is going to be just and human? The answer is you don't know; speaking for Africa, you can only say with Wole Soyinka, you have to crack the nut and take the future between your teeth; and with Albert Camus, himself born into a dying colonial situation and writing under Nazi occupation in Europe: 'We have chosen to accept human justice with its terrible imperfections, careful only to correct it through a desperately maintained honesty.'

—*Graduation Address to the University of the Witwatersrand, 1980*

HOW SHALL WE LOOK AT

EACH OTHER THEN?

Our poet, Mongane Wally Serote, writes:

> *So we shall have buried apartheid—*
> *How shall we look at each other then,*
> *How shall we shake hands . . .*
> *What shall we look like*
> *When that sunrise comes*
> *. . . I ask my people*
> *For we have said*
> *South Africa belongs to all*
> *who live in it.*

And an American analyst of world problems wrote recently:

The choice of what to remember . . . is also a way of recommending choices for the present and the future.

There is a lot of forgetting to do, in South Africa. Yet it should not begin before we face what we are in relation to what we wish to become. Progressive forces in our country are pledged to one of the extraordinary events in world social history: the complete reversal of everything that, for centuries, has ordered the lives of all our people, under all the successive governmental avatars of racism—conquest, colonialism, white republicanism—and that has culminated, again and again, in violence.

We know we have to face the kind of legacy, in terms of human relations, apartheid is leaving us. There is, there will be, an aftermath which can't be tackled *without* majority rule under a bill of rights, but which won't evanesce because of these legal victories over oppression. Just as there are people physically maimed by the struggle between white power and black liberation, there is psychological, behavioural damage that all of us in South Africa have been subject to in some degree, whether we know it or not, whether we are whites who have shut eyes and electronically-controlled gates on what was happening to blacks, or whether we are blacks who have been transported and dumped where the government wished, tear-gassed and shot, detained, forced into exile, or have left to join the liberation army which came into being when no other choice remained. Violence has become the South African way of life.

Violence has been with us a long, long time as a pure expression of racism. In its latest avatars, it is still surely a manipulation of that same racism: an end product of old colonialist ideas of divide and rule in the sophisticated Verwoerdian version of grab and rule—take the land and make kinglets of those given a backing of white government's power in ethnic enclaves. But more of that later.

Does violence imply hate? Personally, I'm prepared to say that hatred towards whites—and in the extreme conditions of racism in South Africa—has been and is rare among South African blacks. I have lived here all my life, I have been in many situations where hate could have revealed itself, I have talked in open mood with many people, when we have been sober and when we have had our inhibitions loosened by a drink or two: I have seen and read much—and, yes, I've met bitterness, hard words, but hate—so unmistakable, so frightening, has not been there.

Hate kills. It is ugly to have to quantify deaths. But how many white civilians have been killed by black Freedom Fighters between 1990 and the time when the liberation movement resorted to arms in 1961?

Sixty-six.

The precise figure comes from no less an authority than Major-General Herman Stadler, given in August 1990.

The figure for black civilians killed by whites, beginning, if you like, with the Sharpeville massacre in 1960, runs into many thousands; no-one really knows how many, counting deaths in detention along with those brought about by direct police action.

And now we have four thousand contemporary deaths in which black people have killed one another. These kinds of bloody disputes, described by the media as 'black on black violence', with the implication that such violence must be tribal, are, we know, basically political. To put it bluntly but not simplistically, without the migratory labour system where, in single-sex hostels, thousands of men have no bonding but herd-bonding, without the chaotic overcrowding of black townships and squatter camps where these men are set down among people who themselves have been herded together, dispossessed under the Group Areas act of the places where they used to live, the unbearable tensions that arise over anything—often something as basic as the communal use of a water tap—would not come about. Without the division of the country into so-called national states, which the de Klerk government has abandoned as a failure without being energetic about seeking to undo the damage that has been done, there would have been no personal power base of a Chief Mangosuthu Buthelezi from which a private army, strengthened by the third fist of white extremists and mercenaries, could attack trade unionists and the mass democratic movement, inevitably drawing counter-violence from these, and spilling over into a Terror comprised of further partisan tensions among the surrounding populace.

But the habit of violence has been instilled, and this is a problem we know will be inherited by a new South Africa. The vocabulary of violence has become the common speech of both black and white.

Among whites, with the phenomenon of no less than seventy white extremist organizations (some consisting of a handful of people, others of considerable numbers), I would say that hate *is* the motive of violence. We have seen the disgusting banners these people hold up. We have heard the venom towards blacks shouted under the sign of a new version of the swastika. But apart from this white minority, I believe destructive emotions among whites stop short of hate. For fear does not always go inextricably with hate. And the prevailing emotion among whites is fear; fear of retribution for all that has been done to blacks by whites' forefathers, by governments for whom they themselves have voted; for all that they themselves have done by their own actions and—for their silence, their turning away with closed eyes. Fear of losing privilege; if they can be convinced that they won't lose their lives, they yet see themselves about to be skinned of their privileges of being white. But subconsciously they understand hate as the useless emotion it is—

even if this is understood only in terms of what it could do for them, now: precisely nothing.

They channel their fears more pragmatically. In Giuseppe di Lampedusa's famous novel about the decaying Sicilian aristocracy's tactics during the invasion of Garibaldi's republican troops, one of the princelings says: 'If we want things to stay as they are, things will have to change.' In other words, 'Let's make all the changes necessary to hold off losing our privilege.'

We have to learn to see the paradox there.

Resentment is a potential source of violence among us. Resentment, while distinct from hate, distorts and maims human relations. Resentment comes to the privileged after privilege has been justly taken away; resentment is something that has been with the oppressed all their lives, for generations, and that is likely to remain, blown upon by freedom to glow from under the ashes of past oppression, in the attitudes of many blacks towards whites, after apartheid. We shall have to find ways other than violence to resolve both kinds of resentment.

Much is made, in the outside world and at home, among those in opposition to real change or determined to manage it for their own ends, of cultural differences as a source of violence between blacks and whites in South Africa. But if we turn away from the obsession with group categories and the neglect of everyday, individual relationships upon which, in the end, human relationships depend, we find that ways of life, mores and manners forced upon us by apartheid laws, down to the details of which toilet we could use, and by custom, to the grading of butchers' meat between general cuts, 'servants' meat' and 'pets' meat'—these ways of life that we've been born to have created differences between black and white that are neither the product of any separate tradition, religion, etc., nor a matter of ethnic temperament.

It is racist politics and laws which have caused morbid mutations, in favour of violence, in our behaviour. We must recognize this. Race has become a catch-all for every form of personal
conflict, at home, in the work-place, in the street. All ordinary,
individual human failings become attributable to the race of the
culprit in societies where people are defined by colour. All of us,
black and white, are caught out at some time in this kind of
conditioned thinking. Part of the anxiety among whites to have
minority rights—group rights—written into a new constitution despite (or in my view, in contradiction of) a bill of rights
to guard the individual, comes from these morbid mutations
which have come about among us. Whites surely need to realize
that group rights would categorise them still within the dead
apartheid structure, single them out, perpetuate the memory of
racism and lead to the possibility of continuing violence?

I welcome this chance to open discussion of the historical
and psychological problems of violence we inherit from the
past, and to face them not as some immutable curse but as
forms of conditioning we can *un*learn, learn to shed, casting the
skin of the old skin differences from which a dictatorship of the
skin, a political system, a system of religious beliefs, a bizarre
social order, was devised, and from which so much suffering has
come.

The perceptions of others about violence in general in the
contemporary world may give us some helpful perspectives. At
a recent conference in Norway it became clear that we delegates
fell into two distinct categories of priority in dealing with violent conflict. There were those subjectivists who believe that a
spiritual change of heart is the basis of peaceful resolution, and
those, the objectivists—among whom I numbered—who
believe that the basis has to be just economic conditions. Václav
Havel said violent hatred ' . . . is a diabolical attribute of the

fallen angel; a state of the spirit that aspires to be God, that may even think it *is* God, and cannot be.' Love one another or perish. But can you love me while I have a full stomach and you are hungry? The American economist John Kenneth Galbraith said, 'Hard, visible circumstance defines reality. Out of poverty comes conflict.' And Elena Bonner said, 'Moral concepts are lovely, but the key is governing things by just law.'

I believe we must create material justice before we can hope to eliminate the kind of violence that has become a tragic habit in South Africa. Given that base, I believe there is a good chance of decent relations between black and black, black and white in our country, whatever languages they speak, whatever their ethnic origins may be. For I can think of no other country in Africa where, in spite of our extraordinary racism, a comparable proportion of people of all races have committed themselves to the black struggle for freedom, recognizing it as their own. Now we need a politics that will nurture material justice before we can hope to live in peace. A new constitution, new laws must change the economic circumstances of the majority; healing can take place only on that honesty of purpose. And that healing will need all the patience and tolerance I believe many blacks and whites are prepared to give it.

—1990

29 OCTOBER 1989

—A BEAUTIFUL DAY, COM

———◆———

The gawky tripods of television cameras stalked the green of the field at Soccer City, photographers in their many-pocketed vests imported from Banana Republic stores in New York took aim from contorted positions along the curving tiers of people who were there to participate and not to report. But I saw notebooks and even the reverse sides of posters balanced on knees while hands carefully managed ball-pens.

For all of us who shared a sense of occasion without precedent in our lives there must have been differences in the lens of experience, memory, through which we saw ourselves and others in that vast congress. Not even the novelist in me can imagine what the senses of Walter Sisulu and his wife, Albertina, were receiving as they walked round the perimeter of the field, protected from the sun by vivid Congress of South African Trade Unions umbrellas—a process like a *durbar*, exposed to the single, enormous throat of joy opening around them. And how did Ahmed Kathrada see the faces, caps, flags, saluting raised fists, banners, massed as bright spores grown over the huge amphitheater? What were Elias Motsoaledi and Wilton Mkwayi thinking—all these released prisoners of conscience moving along this strangest of ceremonial aisles, that led around a soccer field from decades of prison and silence to a rostrum under the sky where they would speak, and be heard by thousands, and the words would circle away by satellite, beyond the miserable range of police helicopters?

Sitting beside me was a boy of about ten or eleven. He was eating chips and held tightly a length of wire with a home-made ANC flag tied to it. What was he feeling? Was he the kid I saw, enjoying the Sunday outing, the band and singers who prepared us for the arrival of the leaders, or was he a child who was more mature, in his terrible experience of facing police guns, than I—old enough to be his grandmother—will ever be?

For me, the context of what I was seeing and hearing expanded its meaning, both from within myself and in the actual physical setting. The stadium, although it belongs to Soweto, is not embedded in its endless streets. It is outside, on the open veld. Its great bowl is partly sunk in the ground; I could see the pale yellow mountains of gold-mine waste dumps rising beyond its rim, and between them, the towers of Johannesburg, gauzy in the heat haze, but present. An entire history was displayed there, no vision but concrete reality; a history in which this Sunday was some sort of culmination of justice—certainly not the final one, but surely the first. There were the mine dumps thrown up by the blacks' labour; there was the greatest city in Africa, built with the whites' profit from that labour; and here, in this stadium, were black leaders, incarcerated for a generation, emerged at last to claim what belongs to their people.

I've been attending courts at which the right to this claim
has been arraigned as criminal, for many years. The first time
was in 1956, the first major treason trial. In the sixties I heard
Nelson Mandela make his speech from the dock—become a
classic liberation text—when he was sentenced to life imprisonment. I was there when Bram Fischer spoke as a prisoner and
not as a distinguished advocate, repudiating the right of an
apartheid court to administer justice, and went away to imprisonment ended only by death. Last December I was honoured to
give evidence in mitigation in the Delmas treason trial of
United Democratic Front leaders Patrick Lekota, Popo Molefe,
and others. For me, the sight of the seven leaders whom I
remembered going to prison years ago, now coming out with
the possibility of being greeted as they should be, with the triumphantly open homage of all of us who care for the liberation
of South Africa, was something I privately received as part of
the fulfilment of my life as a South African. I felt this, I write
this, as one of the crowd.

And by the way, there were seventy thousand of us—different figures have been published (South African television
reportedly reduced us to ten thousand . . .)—but I have it from
a soccer official himself, who knows the total capacity of Soccer
City stadium, and from my own evidence of the extent to which
it overflowed that Sunday.

Everyone has remarked on the efficiency—and what's more,
the style and dignity—of the way the rally was arranged and
conducted. I have my own view of that, because I happen to
know that this extraordinary occasion and the gigantic task it
represented was made possible, in the main, by a handful of
people of whom three are my young colleagues in the Congress
of South African Writers: Junaid Ahmed, Raks Seakhoa, and
Menzi Ndaba. The marshals recruited from youth organisations

presented a very different picture of black youths from that in the minds of whites who see them as stone-throwers and arsonists. Armed only with patience and friendliness, addressing everyone as "Com" ("Comrade": in our passion, in the mass democratic movement, for humanising grandiose terms into diminutives), they kept firm order and didn't find it demeaning to tidy away discarded paper cups.

Who were the people who made up the enormous gathering-in of celebrants? Outside the stadium were what looked, from the height of the exit stairways, like a residential quarter of curved-roof habitations: they were parked buses. They came from all over the country, some travelling all night, and they had brought the majority of the crowd. The form of transport was confirmation of what I remarked in the stadium; this crowd was overwhelmingly black working-class. I didn't see many in the smart outfits of the black middle class; someone said they had stayed away because of the threats of white extremists to attack the rally. There were white faces dotted about in every section of the stands; grey heads of some of the pioneer leftists, Black Sash women, representatives of the National Union of South African Students, the Johannesburg Democratic Action Committee, people representing other radical or progressive groups or simply their own solidarity with the ANC; even a new association of Afrikaner democrats announced last week. No, we whites didn't 'stand out' at all.

Nobody, least of all the released leaders, thinks the continuation to liberation is going to be easy. But whatever is to come, Sunday was a beautiful day, Com. It made a definition of beauty new to me: harmony and trust between human beings of all colours, peace in a gathering huge as a soccer crowd.

—October 1989

MANDELA:

WHAT HE MEANS TO US

━━◦◦◦━━

Let us now praise famous men

Nelson Mandela is *the* famous man, today. One of the few who, in contrast with those who have made our twentieth century infamous for fascism, racism, and war, will mark it as an era that achieved advancement for humanity. So will his name live in history, the context in which he belongs to the world.

Of course, we South Africans are part of that context and share this perception of him. But he belongs to us, and—above all—we belong to him on another and different level of experience.

There are those who knew him in childhood in his home, the Transkei, and see, beneath the ageing face formed by extraordinary experiences of Underground existence and imprisonment, the soft contours of a lively youth unaware of the qualities within him beyond a commonplace appetite for life. There are those who knew him as a colleague with whom they shared food when he, as a black man, could not be served in a restaurant; as a young lawyer whose very presence in court was challenged by white presiding magistrates. There are Freedom Fighters who sacrificed their lives and are not with us to match the image of the leader, in the struggle they shared, with the statesman who has brought it to fulfilment. There are those who see, superimposed upon his public appearances, his face in newspapers and on television today, the memory of his face, figure, and bearing as he spoke from the dock when he was given a life sentence for his actions against apartheid, and declared a commitment he has lived up to since, many times, through many dangers: *I have cherished the ideal of a democratic and free society in which all persons live together in harmony and with opportunities. It is an ideal which I hope to live for and achieve. But if needs be, it is an ideal for which I am prepared to die.*

It's a temptation to be anecdotal about Mandela. To speak, each of us who has had even some brief point of contact with him, of the pleasure of being remembered as well as remembering. For this man with the Atlas-like weight of our future borne on his erect shoulders does have what appears to be some kind of mind-reading facility to pick up identities, some card-index mnemonic system (perhaps developed in the long contemplative years in prison) that enables him to recognize people he may not have seen for years, or whom he may have met fleetingly during recent weeks of hand-shaking encounters. But this is no trick of political showmanship. Seemingly insignificant, it is a sign of something profound: a remove from self-centredness; the capacity to live for others that is central to his character.

He moves about the country now and is a flesh-and-blood presence to millions. For twenty-seven years he was imprisoned; in our midst—for Robben Island is in sight of Table Mountain, in Cape Town, and Pollsmoor Prison and the house which was made into a private prison for him, ultimately, are part of the city—and yet, in social terms, entombed. Silenced. Even his image removed; it was forbidden to reproduce his photograph in newspapers or other media.

He could so easily have become legendary, his features recomposed as the ikon of hopes that never would be realized and a freedom that always receded as each wave of resistance within our country was crushed and seemed defeated, and the outside world was indifferent. But the people had a sense of his *enduring what they knew*: the harsh humiliations of prison were everyday experiences to black people under the apartheid pass laws and innumerable other civil restrictions that for generations created a vast non-criminal prison population in South Africa. When he and his colleagues were sent to break stones and pull seaweed out of the Atlantic Ocean, ordinary people among the black population were being hired out by prison authorities as slave farm labour. His people kept him among them in the words of their songs and chants, in the examples of forms of resistance he had passed on to them, and in the demands for his release which were part of the liberation platform, maintained both by leadership in exile and the people themselves, at home. In such news of him that came out of prison, we came to know that his sense of himself was always part of all this, of living it with his people; he received them through prison walls, as they kept him with them.

This double sense was instrinsic to the very stuff of resistance. The strong possibility that he would die in prison was never considered for acceptance. There never was the psychological defeat, for the liberation movement, of his becoming a mythical figure, a Che Guevara, who might reappear someday only in a mystical resurrection on a white horse, since once a personage becomes a myth he has disappeared forever as a leader to take on the present in vulnerable flesh.

Of course, it remains difficult to write of a phenomenon like Mandela in terms other than hagiography. But he is not a god-like figure, despite his enormous popularity—and this popularity, in the era of successful negotiation between black and white, extends in all kinds of directions beyond the trust and reverence in which he is held by blacks and those whites who have been active in liberation from apartheid. I heard on the news while I was writing this that a poll of South African businessmen has revealed that 68 percent wished to see Nelson Mandela as the future president of South Africa . . . Far from assuming a celestial status, Mandela has a quality that is, on the contrary, so fully and absolutely that of a man, the essence of a human being in all the term should mean, could mean, but seldom does. He belongs completely to a real life lived in a particular place and era, and in its relation to the world. He is at the epicentre of our time; ours in South Africa, and yours, wherever you are.

For there are two kinds of leaders. There is the man or woman who creates the self—his/her life—out of the drive of personal ambition, and there is the man or woman who creates a self out of response to people's needs. To the one, the drive comes narrowly from within; to the other, it is a charge of energy that comes of others' needs and the demands these make. Mandela's dynamism of leadership is that he has within him the selfless quality to receive and act upon this charge of energy. He has been a revolutionary leader of enormous courage, is a political negotiator of extraordinary skill and wisdom, a statesman in the cause of peaceful change. He has suffered and survived more than a third of his life in prison and emerged without uttering one word of revenge. He has had many personal family sorrows as a result of his imprisonment. He has borne all this, it is evident, not only because the cause of freedom in South Africa for his people has been the breath of his life, but because he is that rare being for whom the human family is his family. When he speaks of South Africa as the home of all South Africans, black and white, he means what he says. Just as he did when he stood in court and vowed that he was prepared to die for this ideal.

At the rendezvous of victory there is room for all. Mandela's actions and words show he knows that without that proviso there is no victory, for anyone.

—On the occasion of Nelson Mandela's
receiving the Nobel Peace Prize, 1993

THE FIRST TIME

April 27, 1994

Standing in the queue this morning; businessmen in their jogging outfits, nurses in uniform (two, near me, still wearing the plastic mob-caps that cover their hair in the cloistered asepsis of the operating theatre), black women in their Zionist Church outfits, white women and black women who shared the mothering of white and black children winding about their legs, people who had brought folding stools to support their patient old bones, night watchmen just off duty, girl students tossing long hair the way horses switch their tails—here we all were as we have never been. We have stood in line in banks and post offices together, yes, since the desegregation of public places; but until this day there was always the unseen difference between us, far more decisive than the different colours of our skins: some of us had the right that is the basis of all rights, the symbolic X, the sign of a touch on the controls of polity, the mark of citizenship, and others did not. But today we stood on new ground.

The abstract term 'equality' took on materiality as we moved towards the church hall polling station and the simple act, the drawing of an X, that ended over three centuries of privilege for some, deprivation of human dignity for others.

The first signature of the illiterate is the X. Before that there was only the thumb-print, the skin-impression of the powerless. I realized this with something like awe when, assigned by my local branch of the African National Congress to monitor procedures at a polling booth, I encountered black people who could not read or write. A member of the Independent Electoral Commission would guide them through what took on the solemnity of a ritual; tattered identity document presented, hands outstretched under the ultra-violet light, hands sprayed with invisible ink, and meticulously folded ballot paper—a missive ready to be despatched for the future—placed in those hands. Then an uncertain few steps towards a booth, accompanied by the IEC person and one of the various Party agents to make sure that, when the voter said which party he or she wished to vote for, the X would be placed in the appropriate square. Several times I was that Party agent and witnessed a man or woman giving this signature to citizenship. The first time man scratched the mark of his identity, the conscious proof of his existence, on a stone, must have been rather like this.

Nearby in city streets there were still destitute black children sniffing glue as the only substitute for nourishment and care; there were homeless families existing in rigged-up shelters in the crannies of the city. The law places the ground of equality underfoot; it did not feed the hungry or put a roof over the head of the homeless, today, but it changed the base on which

South African society was for so long built. The poor are still there, round the corner. But they are not the Outcast. They no longer can be decreed to be forcibly removed, deprived of land, and of the opportunity to change their lives. They *count*. The meaning of the counting of the vote, whoever wins the majority, is this, and not just the calculation of the contents of ballot boxes.

If to be alive on this day was not Wordsworth's 'very heaven' for those who have been crushed to the level of wretchedness by the decades of apartheid and the other structures of racism that preceded it, standing in line to be living at this hour has been extraordinary. The day has been captured for me by the men and women who couldn't read or write, but underwrote it, at last, with their kind of signature. May it also be the seal on the end of illiteracy, of the pain of imposed ignorance.

April 29, 1994

'J'ai plus de souvenirs que si j'avais mille ans.'

Baudelaire's words. I woke this morning with an over-flowing sense of continuity; today is three days run into one. Voting was still in progress for the first elections ever, in the history of my country, in which everyone, whatever the colour of skin, at last has the franchise.

It's been impossible to think of anything but the experience we are living through; I have not been able to write or even read anything other than newspapers. The second volume of Naguib Mahfouz's wonderful *Cairo Trilogy* lies with a bookmark halfway through the pages. The newspapers' interviews with politicians and people in the streets, the editorial speculation on the outcome of this election—which is not Europe's or America's customary recurrent event of the exchange of power between one party and another within an accepted polity that respects both—are part of the epic of our transformation: to us, prophesy rather than reportage. Forecasts of the results come from the television box as from the mouth of an oracle. I feel that I understand the meaning of 'destiny' for the first time: one of those grandiose quasi-religious concepts I have always regarded with scepticism. But these three days, in which millions of people have moved in those slow queues as pilgrims to their future, carry the weight of the word.

Their procession has continued to pass through my mind, it has no relation to the span of days, it extends through the waiting years, decades, the centuries during which black people have toiled their way on the farms, in the gold and diamond and platinum mines that made the country rich and gave its original inhabitants so little; toiled their way through banishment from their homes because whites wanted their land; risen again from where they had fallen under tear-gas and police batons; buried those who fell before police gun-fire, and gathered again to march in strikes, in mass protest, a generations-long procession on the way—at last, at last!—to the polling booth. I have preferred to think of the inevitable final arrival as a process of history, but call it history or destiny, it has the meaning of people coming into their own. Something ordained, yet only to be achieved by suffering and endurance.

For me, in the queues, there are the black migratory mine-workers with their clay-covered locks and blankets worn like togas I used to see on my way to my convent school in a gold-mining town sixty years ago; there is the old woman who worked in my mother's kitchen and whose cup my mother forbade me to drink from for fear of the contagion of a black skin; there is the ebullient jazz composer, Todd Matshikiza, who was the first black man in whose arms I danced; there is the writer, my other dear friend, Nat Nakasa, who in the despair of exile jumped from a skyscraper window in New York; there is the painter, Gerard Sekoto, who was the Goya of life in the black townships and died, far from home, in Paris. And there are, among whites mingled there, those who gave their lives along with blacks in the trek towards liberation: blue-eyed Afrikaner Bram Fischer serving a life sentence as a revolutionary, dying too soon to see this day, this end of the procession. And in the faces of old black men there is the likeness of Oliver Tambo, the Moses who with Mandela, for so long, first from home and then from exile, led his people out of bondage.

In the image of Tambo also came my change of mood, to celebration. Later in the day I was a guest of Adelaide Tambo, his wife, at the suburban house with its garden and swimming-pool—formerly the jealous preserve of whites—that the African National Congress bought for Tambo to honour and provide him with comfort in the short period between his return from exile and his death in 1993. The place was ringing with joy; a choir, from the segregated black township in the mining district where I was born in the segregated white township, was singing before guests assembled in the house. They sang with the power of the whole body; it was impossible not to begin to move one's muscles and flesh with theirs—the rooms and outer hall were caught up in the current of emotion. Adelaide was regally flamboyant in African robes. Foreign guests of honour— prominent individuals from Europe and the United States, including David Dinkins, former mayor of New York, who have supported the struggle against apartheid—queued (once again) round tables set out with food and drink, and everyone drifted to eat and talk in the garden. The beat of liberation changed again. One of our best bands was playing African jazz, the wild music expressive of the irrepressible embrace of life that never loosened in the grasp of black people, no matter what drudgery and humiliation were there to extinguish their spirit. It's our music; it reconciled black and white, even among those conditioned by racial prejudice, even while the law kept black and white apart, long before reconciliation became official policy. Listening, I wondered how much liberation owes to this language that never lies because it has no words.

We were feasting, as people have done to celebrate fulfilment since before recorded history. In my mind the procession to the polling stations kept unwinding. I thought how what we were celebrating in the garden was the hope that the simple feast of life in peace and in justice before the law might be gained for all the people in that procession; that, at least, at last, 'They shall sit every man under his vine and under his fig-tree' (Micah 4.4).

ACT TWO: ONE YEAR LATER

1. *Accept nothing as true which I did not clearly recognise to be so; that is to say, to avoid carefully precipitation and prejudice, and to accept nothing in my judgments beyond what presented itself so clearly and distinctly to my mind, that I should have no occasion to doubt it.*
2. *Divide each of the difficulties which I examined into as many parts as possible, and might be necessary in order best to resolve them.*
3. *Carry on my reflections in order, starting with those objects that were the most simple and easy to understand, so as to rise little by little, by degrees, to the knowledge of the most complex: assuming an order among those that did not naturally fall into a series.*
4. *Last, in all cases make enumerations so complete and reviews so general that I should be sure of leaving nothing out.*

May I be at all sure that I can follow Descartes' method when gathering together this single year that has taken up within its unique newness all that was held back, accumulating in the conflicting stalemates of the past? It's a toppling wave; twelve months is hardly enough time to regain breath. I'll have a go.

Best for me to begin with Rule 3. The order of my reflection cannot be chronological, but rises to mind idiosyncratically, generally, the public events see-sawing with the private ones, so the personal value system has to be sorted out from the politico-social one. It is simple and easy to enumerate high on the list my own sense of joy when, again and again, I've seen friends whom I've known as exiles, prisoners, hunted occupants of the Underground, now bearing high office and deferred to by international dignitaries, their formerly banned voices quoted in the press and their forbidden faces blooming on the TV screen.

Albie Sachs, maimed by the apartheid government's attempt to kill him, now sitting as a judge on the Constitutional Court. Barbara Masekela, exiled for years, soon to take up an important diplomatic post. Mongane Wally Serote, Freedom Fighter, poet in exile working for the African National Congress around the world, now taking his seat as a duly elected member of parliament. To measure up to Rule 1, here: I accept as true, and clearly recognise to be so, that justice has come about in the person of these individuals, as it has supremely to that ex-political prisoner, now President Nelson Mandela. And justice is sweeter to see than revenge.

When I return to South Africa from abroad, now, I don't step down onto the earth of my old stamping ground, the Transvaal, where I was born, but onto new territory. It's named Gauteng—Place of Gold. The airport itself is renamed. It used to be Jan Smuts Airport; now it is Johannesburg International Airport. The former name—Transvaal—derived, way back, from the geographical boundaries recognised by the Boer Republics: Transvaal—across the Vaal River—was where the water divided the Boer Republic of Orange Free State from its counterpart, the Boer Republic of Transvaal. The former name of the airport commemorated General Jan Smuts, one of the heroes of the white regime, who sat with Churchill, Roosevelt, and Stalin, led South Africa boldly into the war against Nazi racism, but continued to head a racist government back home.

Now Gauteng stoutly asserts not only that there will be no more white republics here, but that their latter-day apartheid counterpart, the slicing of the country into ethnic enclaves, is over, for good. If Place of Gold trails any historical trappings, these commemorate the labour of the black men who brought the underground metal to the surface and made the country rich, as much as the Europeans who made the ore discoveries, supplied the technology, and took the profits.

I've become easily accustomed to the new Johannesburg. But when I've been away and come home, fresh to it, my vision zigzags back to the way it was, for fascinated comparison. I've lived here since 1949, and at most levels that segregation reserved for whites. I've been a struggling young writer, divorced, with a child to support. I've ended up in a beautiful old tin-roofed house with room for my books. But whenever and however I've lived, during the past regimes, it was where no black person could rent a room, a flat, or buy a house.

On to the most complex of what happened. The general public events; still with Rule 3. In the eighties, things began to change. People in other countries tend to think that the elections in April 1994 achieved this from zero, overnight. It was not so. During the eighties, even while the state repression resorted to vile and savage hit-squad tactics to assassinate liberation leaders, the theatres, cinemas, and restaurants were declared open to everybody. Blacks could sit down to eat. Public transport was desegregated. Blacks could ride. Although a lot of legalistic pussy-footing to retain residential segregation remained, it was ignored by the growing confidence of black people moving into white high-density areas, and white landlords eager to fill vacancies where whites had retreated to the suburbs. Back in the city, the white government's lack of interest or success in providing transport to serve blacks in their daily to-and-fro between the white city and the black ghettoes was replaced by a most disorderly but effective form of transport provided by thousands of minibuses owned by black private enterprise.

These were the concessions made, and the changes helplessly accepted by the last days of apartheid, holed up in its bunker but determined not to swallow the cyanide capsule.

Rule 2. It would take more pages than the quota I've given myself to divide each of the difficulties I ought to examine—or rather my own reaction to them—and to resolve all within myself. There is a shambling off the scene of the white Right-wing extremists whom I feared, last year, when they used bombs in an attempt to prevent the elections from taking place; by contrast, the continuing trouble-making of Mangosuthu Buthelezi that was to be expected; and the unexpected dangers of Winnie Mandela's will to power. To turn back the clock is not something I should ever wish to do, with exception in respect of Winnie Mandela. I wish we could re-run her emergence, hand in hand with Nelson Mandela, from his prison, so that this extraordinary woman whom I have known and admired through many early years could see that if she had kept beside him she would have been no mere consort, as her ambition perhaps misled her to believe. He is the greatest statesman and leader in the world, today— a fulfilment of everything we could have hoped for, from him, on the 27th April last year. The couple would have doubled the impact, a unique combination in the world and our part of it. That was where her power lay.

A difficulty to be faced in my mind is what is known as labour 'unrest'. We have had a great number of strikes this year, and we shall have many more to come. The most important ones are those in the mines and related industries, because these are bound up with the colonial-established employment practice of migratory labour that, in turn, is related to the recurrent violence which spills from the frustration of hostel living conditions to adjacent black communities. This strife is often fuelled by the political ambitions of the former Good Black Man of the apartheid government, Buthelezi, recklessly stirring the power-brew of ethnic differences. Other workers have come out on strike—supermarket employees, transport drivers, even gravediggers.

These actions are deplored because they affect production (not the gravediggers, of course . . .) and growth of the economy, but we have to remind ourselves: under the old regime, police, dogs, and guns were the only answer to workers' assertion of their rights. Yet workers' actions are represented in the press at home and abroad as the sure sign that things are going wrong in our country; overseas investors withdraw their heads into their corporate shells.

A failure of democracy that workers go on strike?

What do we want—the 'industrial peace' of our old police state?

The consequences of these industrial actions are one of the heritages of apartheid that will continue to plague us, for a long time. While rightfully taking up demands for a living wage, safe working conditions in mines and factories, a say in management, and the opening of company books to scrutiny, the trade unions have not yet educated their members on the relation between production, profits, and wages. And the bosses have not wished to educate themselves on the relation between workers and bosses in a democracy; after decades where all you had to do was bring in a load of migratory workers and set them before the right levers, like Chaplin in *Modern Times,* the men in the boardroom find it difficult to understand that in a democracy there can be a chance for industrial peace only if the workers are represented in policy-making and management decisions. The next issue of contention to arise surely will be between workers and government: the exhilarating gale of change is blowing privatisation our way, if we want to attract the foreign investment we need.

Some of what we apprehensively anticipated to be the most complex (Rule 3 again) in the series of events in our first year has happily disproved fear, for me. The opening of the 1995 school year in January was one such.

Here was the transformation of our world beginning at the *real beginning*: with children. Large numbers of black children—both those who live with their parents in the city as part of the exodus from black townships, and those whose parents brought them that morning from those segregated townships—were registered at what had been white schools. It wasn't necessary to have these children escorted by police or army, as happened when schools were desegregated in the U.S.A. There occurred less than a handful of incidents where white people gathered in protest. Of course, the majority of black children in the urban and rural ghettoes apartheid created are still without enough schools or teachers—a vast lack. But each time, at the end of a school day, I pass a school near where I live and see black and white children streaming out of class, the small boys scuffling joyfully, the girls giggling together, I know that something at the very base of our lives has changed, from the shameful, to the genesis of human fulfilment.

Early this year I attended the inaugural sitting of our Constitutional Court—the first such body in our history. The case was brought by two men on death row, on the grounds that the death penalty violates South Africa's new Constitution. It was a test case of tremendous significance to the Constitution as final arbiter of individual human rights. Among the judges, black and white, was Albie Sachs, the liberation activist whose arm was blown off and one eye blinded by a car bomb placed to kill him by the apartheid government's hit squads; he, who might be thought to want to see assassins die, was eloquent for abolition of the death penalty. The court finally declared it a contravention of the Constitution and it has been abolished. Eighty percent of whites and forty-nine percent of blacks had wanted it retained. Judge President Arthur Chaskalson said, 'This court cannot allow itself to be diverted from its duty to act as an independent arbiter of the Constitution by the public'. We now have, and need to have, this kind of protection of individual rights where we had so few. Those who kill will go to prison for life; the state will not become a murderer.

We have other kinds of murderers among us; political murderers who have never been brought to justice. President Mandela recently signed into law a Truth and Reconciliation Commission. It is a country of reconciliation's preferred alternative to Germany's Nuremberg trials or Chile's blanket amnesty. Those who come forward and confess fully what they did and why, in the past, may be granted forgiveness and in some cases amnesty. It's going to be a process full of doubts and difficulties, both for the perpetrators of ghastly deeds and for the families of those they killed or maimed. But it is surely the way to deal with the past of a people who have to live with it, together; a dedicated move towards making South Africa a human place to live in, today.

The injunction (Rule 4) to be sure to leave nothing out? I couldn't attempt to follow that because, in the period of a single year, so much remains to be redressed, so much has had to be

'left out' for another year; years. What is before my eyes is that
the streets of this city, Johannesburg, where I live, are now
totally transformed. A perpetual crowd scene on a Cecil B.
DeMille scale has taken over what was a swept, empty stage on
which a few self-appointed leading actors performed for one
another. The pavements are a market where your progress is a
step-dance between pyramids of fruit and vegetables, racks of
second-hand jeans, spreads of dog-eared paperback lives from
Marx to Mandela and Monroe, rickety tables set with peanuts,
sweets, sunglasses, backyard concoctions labelled Chanel and
Dior, hair straighteners, Swatches and earrings. Traffic fumes
are spiced by the smell of *boerewors*, a greasy farm sausage that is
as much our national dish as thick mealie-meal, the African
polenta, for on every corner there are carts frying circles of gut-
encased meat over gas burners. You can have your shoes re-soled
while you stand in your socks; you can even have your hair cut,
right there. Like everyone else who has a car, I have had to
acquire new skills as a driver after forty-seven years on the road:
the minibuses we call combis—a combination between a bus
and a taxi—stop on request signalled by a raised finger, anywhere and everywhere. You have to be ready with the foot on
the brake and a quick swerve to make it to the parallel lane, and
usually the lane is full, anyway.

The city centre is dirty, yes. That private white club, that
stage-set for principal actors only, was not designed for non-
members, for the use of the crowd, the entire population of this
city. The dainty bins overflow with trash. And perhaps there is
even an unconscious euphoria among black people, in showing
you may toss your cigarette pack and a Coke can, even your old
T-shirt, onto what white people kept so tidy, for themselves
alone. It will take some time before people want to have clean
streets because they have now claimed them. I use the word

'unconscious' of this careless abandon in the streets because there is so little general resentment of whites, in black South Africans. I reflect on this as I write: when I walk about Johannesburg these days I don't do so as a white among blacks, I'm not conscious of this at all, it's not there in the eyes, in the gait of the people as they approach or pass me. And if we happen to bump into one another, before I can apologise, the other will say, 'Sorry, ma-Gogo'—*I apologise, grandmother*—in respect for my grey hair. . . .

There are muggings, house robberies, and hijacks to fear, oh yes. And although it is easy for me to say these are the hazards of city life in many countries, certainly (but not only) the developing, post-colonial ones, it is a statistical fact that our city ranks very high on the crime scale. In one of the paradoxes of freedom, our country is no exception. For all those years of apartheid, we were isolated from the world, rightly shunned; now we are accepted with open arms and we ourselves are also open to arrival from other countries of drug dealers and scam-men, and on a humbler but nevertheless damaging level, illegal immigrants from as far afield as Nigeria, Korea, and China, who compete with our own unemployed in the struggle to earn and eat.

The vast number of unemployed we inherited from the apartheid regime, like the millions in need of houses and schools, have created a vocation of crime, with, as apprentices, homeless street children. It's a Dickensian situation apartheid bequeathed us and foreigners exacerbate, ironically, in our freedom. It's an inheritance not only from the years of apartheid since 1948, but of the more than three and a half centuries of colonial racist rule under different names.

What has our Government of National Unity been able to do about this inheritance, this social malediction, in the short months of its existence in power?

I am incredulous when people in the outside world call us to account in the quantitative terms *they* have decided. How many houses have we built? Too few, yes, too few, we are well aware. But how many do these South Africa watchers calculate, of the thousands required by several million shack and slum dwellers, could be built in a year?

This is not a game of Monopoly, where a house is a counter you put down on a chosen square.

Do they realize that land has to be legally acquired, in relation to where people have their work-places, that electricity and water reticulation have to be installed where during apartheid they never existed, that—above all—banks have to be negotiated into providing low-cost housing loans for people who, because they were black and low-income earners, never before were eligible for bonds? These preparations are what takes up time before a brick is laid. The fact that in the region where I live eighty thousand existing houses have been connected to electricity may mean little to you, who have been taking for granted electrical power ever since you were grown enough to reach a switch; but to people who live in those eighty thousand houses, touching a switch is indeed the beginning of a new life: let there be light.

For myself, I have been troubled by some unforeseen turns of events, this year, but I have been neither disappointed nor disillusioned; it's been a year of awesome achievement, set against what preceded it for generations, here.

To maintain a healthy balance, of course, I quote Leibniz's gibe, that Descartes' Rules were 'like the precepts of some chemist; take what you need and do what you should, and you will get what you want.'

Well, I continue to believe it shall be so.

—1995

THE ESSENTIAL DOCUMENT

Everyone who ponders the Universal Declaration of Human Rights inevitably will give particular attention to those Articles that pertain to circumstances with which he or she is personally involved. For me as a writer, Article 19—Freedom of Expression—has a special significance. But this is not a professional privilege that seeks exclusive protection: literature is one of the most enduring means by which ideas cross frontiers and become universal, but freedom of expression, to impart and receive information 'through any media', is the first condition of freedom in civilised governance. Suppression by censorship, banning, imprisonment, and even edicts of death continue to exist in many countries, imposed by both secular and religious authorities. Article 19 established these means as a primary contravention of everyone's birthright to read, to listen, to regard, and speak out.

Article 26 is fundamental to Article 19: its Clauses 1 and 2 declare: 'Everyone has the right to education', 'Education shall be directed to the full development of the human personality'. Freedom of expression is an empty phrase unless education equips every individual with freedom of the word, the ability to read and write. Although the right to literacy surely is implied in Article 26, it is not specifically named. I believe it ought to be. This Article brings the hope of justice to the millions excluded—by ignorance which is no fault of their own—from participation and benefit in the making of our world.

For me, the most important Article of the Universal Declaration of Human Rights has no number, is not an Article at all. It is a paragraph of the Preamble. 'Whereas it is essential, if man is not to be compelled to have recourse, as a last resort, to *rebellion against tyranny and oppression*, that human rights should be protected by the rule of law.' (My italics).

I have lived through a time in my own country, South Africa, when this 'last resort' compelled the majority of the people to turn to rebellion, first in the form of civil disobedience and passive resistance and finally in the form of armed struggle, against tyranny and oppression that denied them human rights. I have seen how to be compelled to take this last resort not only brings tragic self-sacrifice and suffering to those who assume the burden, even though freedom is finally achieved as a result, but has long-term consequences which threaten the democracy so attained.

When people are deprived over years of any recourse to the provisions of civil society as a means of seeking redress for their material and spiritual deprivations, they *lose the faculty* of using the law when, at last, such recourse is open to them. The result of this conditioning now is fashionably called 'the culture of violence'; an oxymoron, for culture implies enlightenment, to aim towards attaining the fullness of life, not its destruction.

The tactics of a desperate liberation struggle are all that many people know how to employ. In my country, students dissatisfied with the performance of their teachers retaliate by destroying the equipment of their own schools. Taxi-bus owners, in dispute over transport routes each considers his exclusively, attack one another at gunpoint. Workers forcibly occupy managers' offices and destroy plants as protest against unsatisfactory working conditions and low pay. It takes time and education in, understanding of, the protection of human rights, for a formerly oppressed people to learn to use this protection through the means provided, in civil societies, by the law. Students had no structures to deal with their grievances, before. The means of settling disputes by forming a code for the transport industry was not open to, offered no peaceful resolution to those who had no civil rights of any kind. The denial of the right to form trade unions, over many years, meant that workers' violent reactions to their problems were the only ones that brought results in the political liberation struggle. The paths by which people have the right to be protected by the rule of law, not persecuted by its wrongful application, have to be learned. It is in this that the Universal Declaration of Human Rights is and shall remain the essential document, the touchstone, the creed of humanity that surely sums up all other creeds directing human behavior if we are to occupy this world together now and in the twenty-first century.

—1997

AS OTHERS SEE US

There is nothing more presumptuous than a foreigner telling other people what is wrong with their country. I know how I react when pundits who are not South African make flip judgments of our problems on the basis of the slim experience of visits to our country. This does not mean that a reasoned, critical look is not useful; just that the onlooker understands not most, but only half of the game. So it is right that I provide my modest credentials for an opinion on race relations in the U.S.A. in contrast to race relations in my own country—relations I have been part of since birth.

I have visited America once a year or more since the 1950s, usually only for several weeks but twice for several months, spent in New York and Cambridge, with forays to the Midwest, the West Coast, and the South. I began in the McCarthy era and have gathered my impressions through the eras of Martin Luther King, Jr., Stokely Carmichael, Andy Young, Louis Farrakhan, and your roster of presidents up to the present incumbent. In my early visits as a young writer I mixed in an easy fashion with a good number of my peers, black men and women whose interests in the arts and in Africa coincided with mine. I remember parties in Queens, welcoming visits to homey apartments, jazz evenings in Harlem not as a gaping tourist but as an individual sharing the leisure diversion of new-found friends themselves. These were not people with big names; all of us were starting out.

As time went by, on subsequent visits to the U.S., I found I was meeting fewer and fewer black Americans. Those that I did meet—and much enjoyed—were Du Bois's Talented Tenth: Harry Belafonte, Charlayne Hunter-Gault, Jamaica Kincaid, Randall Robinson, Toni Morrison, Henry Louis Gates and Cornel West, for example.

While housed in an apartment adjacent to a student residence at Harvard, in 1995, when I gave the Charles Eliot Norton Lectures, almost the only black Americans I met were through the efforts of Skip Gates. The Talented Tenth again. At the homes of my white American friends, people to whom colour truly means nothing, I now find I meet blacks from Africa, but rarely a black American. Whites from Africa who came from active anti-racist backgrounds, and now live in the States, have no black men and women among their friends. Why? A paradox, since back home in South Africa they mixed in tough friendship with blacks, and were totally accepted by them, under conditions that made this difficult, to say the least. The reason seems to be that black Americans do not want to mix with whites, however much compatibility is beckoning to be recognized. The old, old answer I think not only survives but seems to have grown in bitterness, for reasons (of economics and opportunity?) Americans know best: when you have been so long rejected, your collective consciousness tells you that the open door, open arms, have come too late. You assert your self-respect only by saying 'no'. No no no: I read that playwright August Wilson wants black theatre for *blacks only*—black writers, actors, audiences. If even the doors of the arts are slammed shut, how shall people find their common humanity? And how to live together, in the end, without it? This theatre is Greek tragedy where wars and violence become the only means of communication, the curse of gods on humans.

Why does self-respect, identity, rest on this ancient and terrible tragedy of white rejection of black?

One has to look at race relations in South Africa for an explanation of the U.S.A.'s realities. Over three hundred and fifty years of oppression and racist exploitation unequalled in place or time, black South Africans nevertheless have had their own earth under their feet. Despite neglect in official education, their languages have remained intact as mother tongues. Their names are their own ancestral names. Nothing—neither cruel apartheid denigration nor liberal paternalism—has destroyed their identity. *They know who they are.* In relations with whites, now that everyone is equal before the law, they do not have to say 'no' in order to assert pride of identity and self-respect. It is for the average white to discover, earn, and affirm a valid identity in a society with a black majority. There are those whites to whom this is anathema, but surprising numbers who followed the white flock in racism before are making the adjustment. What matter that the process begins as pragmatism. Groups of extremists who cannot adjust will die out with the present middle-aged generation, I believe. And as for those whites who threw in their lot with the black struggle—they are recognized as brothers and sisters and are active in all areas of reconstruction: they are long accustomed to contributing under the direction of blacks.

Unemployment, inequalities in employment opportunities are a heritage of the hopelessly inadequate, segregated education of blacks under apartheid. There is frustration, over this, among blacks, but at the same time black empowerment is a reality moving both at government level (in the civil service and police, more slowly than one would wish, but there are valid reasons in the problems of transition) and the new black private sector. There, black empowerment is moving boldly into the white enclaves round the stock market. If the black entrepreneurs are in some way a home-grown product out of black poverty, like the 'Tough Love Crowd' of successful black American capitalists, the neo-conservatists who advocate unsparing self-criticism as the way to empower blacks, the resemblance ends there. Black South Africans 'climbing the corporate ladder', because of their records of active participation in the liberation struggle, including political detention and imprisonment in many cases, can rightfully maintain their brotherhood with the masses, and defy any questioning of their motives in empowering their people through infiltration of capitalist enterprises within a state where capitalist exploitation was allied with racism. While some say they are betraying the revolution, others see these moves as a necessary phase of struggle: first came the political kingdom, now comes the economic one, to be fought, inevitably, on white economic supremacy's home ground. Lack of capital inhibits these entrepreneurs; they have to borrow finance from whites, but are alert to the way the balance must be precariously held, the frontier of black ownership must be pushed hard and continuously against shareholdings that still entrench white economic power.

In the South African theatre, a cross-pollination of European experimental dramatic structures and African resources of mime, living experiences, shared body-language with whites produces a theatre that is non-racial not only in mixed casting that reflects the tensions and truth of our mixed society, but also in that 'black' plays and 'white' plays are recognized as opportunities opening to each the experience of the other. And all are welcome in the audience.

It is unfortunate to have to say it: history is against you, in the U.S.A. Alas, Martin Luther King is dead and you have no Nelson Mandela. White Americans cannot give back to blacks a stolen and lost identity; black Americans are reluctant to accept that it cannot be found in an avatar of apartheid in reverse. They are Americans, and whether whites like it or not, and whether blacks like it or not, a common destiny has to be worked out. This is not simple, in South Africa either, but in my observation and participation we are doing rather better than the U.S.A., despite our staggering problems of poverty, unemployment, and vast number of the homeless, a legacy from the apartheid regime.

As Wislawa Szymborska, the Polish Nobel Laureate poet, writes: 'We know how to divide ourselves. But to put ourselves together?'

—1997

LABOUR WELL

THE TEEMING EARTH

The poor are always with us.

> The eradication of poverty.

These are the poles of perception, the oppositions of the phenomenon of want.

The poor are always with us.

The first is ancient, an implied acceptance of a destined lot, everyone conditioned by class (each in his place), by religion (the meek shall inherit the earth), to be content to have no place and inherit nothing.

The eradication of poverty.

The second proposition refuses to accept poverty as part of human destiny. The United Nations General Assembly's designation of the International Decade for the Eradication of Poverty is a *mission* statement in the true sense. It is surely the boldest expression of faith in human endeavour ever made? It comes from the most representative body in the world. It posits perhaps the greatest human advancement ever embarked upon, an adventure greater than any attempted in the progress of humankind since we could define ourselves as such. And most important, it asserts convincing proof that the goal could be attainable.

Beginning last year, the United Nations Development Programme has launched an exhaustive, world-wide initiative to debunk poverty as destiny; with its partners, the United Nations system, organizations of civil society, academic institutions, the private sectors and international donor community, research has been produced which identifies the extent and nature of poverty in its many forms—and destiny is not one of them.

I do not propose to cite the statistics of the world of want. They are all there, devastating, in the invaluable publications of the United Nations Development Programme—the staggering material facts of race, racial prejudice, political and social administration, geography, gender, ethnicity, agricultural practice, technological practice, industrial production, health services—everything—from the drying up of a stream to the closing down of an arms factory—that produces the phenomena of poverty as lived by the world's 1.3 billion poor.

When you read this evidence of physical, mental, and spiritual deprivation, you can reach only one conclusion: poverty is a trap. Brought about by many factors other than the obvious ones you may always have had in mind, poverty is the nadir of disempowerment.

It is a disempowerment that has existed and does exist in democracies as well as dictatorships, links them, in a way we are reluctant to have to admit. The ballot box of free and fair elections has failed to empower the poor in most of the democratic countries. The dictatorship of the people failed to do so in most countries of the Soviet empire. And since the fall of Commu-

nism, the West's claim of freeing those countries to the establishment of a market economy and prosperity means nothing to
the old people who now beg in the streets of Moscow, as the
homeless do in the streets of cities of the only great power left
in the world, the United States of America. In Brazil, in
Argentina, in Africa, in India, in Bangladesh—where in this
world except for the small welfare states of the north, are there
not people in the nadir of poverty? No need to enter into ideological differences, no need to make any value judgments, here:
each country has produced—or failed to end—the shameful
human end-product, poverty.

What is a decade—in terms of centuries of acceptance, *the
poor are always with us?*

Our answer surely is that the world now has the knowledge,
the scientific and technological ability to do away with most of
the causes of poverty, and to turn around the consequences of
causes it cannot prevent. There are identified practical means:
what is needed is the money and commitment of governments,
regional, national, and bodies of world governance, to co-
operate and carry out these means. And what is needed to bring
this about is a roused awareness and admittance among the peoples of the world that whether there is proved to be life on Mars,
and whether you may conduct your affairs electronically without leaving your armchair, the new century is not going to be a
new century *at all* in terms of the progress of humanity if we
take along with us acceptance of the shameful shackles of the
past—over a billion men, women, and children in poverty,
eighty-two countries unable to produce or buy sufficient food
for their population—and we offer only charity, that palliative
to satisfy the conscience and keep the same old system of haves
and have-nots quietly contained.

In view of this need for roused awareness, I think it is useful for us to consider: How do different people conceive poverty? How do they think about it? Historically, where did it begin?

In prehistory early humans lived by what we would call now a subsistence economy: you hunted, you gathered, and when these resources of your group ran out in one place, you moved on; only nature discriminated, making one area more salubrious than another, but there was space enough to make of this an advantage rather than a deprivation. It was with the arrival of surplus value that the phenomenon of rich and poor began; with the cultivation of the valleys of the Euphrates and the Nile, when food was grown and could be stored instead of foraged and hunted, able to satisfy only short-term needs. As soon as there was more than sufficient unto the day, those who grew more than they could eat became the haves, while those whose harvest provided no surplus became the have-nots.

Basically, nothing has changed since then. Except that it is no longer possible for societies to move on from one disadvantaged environment to a more salubrious one—the colonial era of the European powers was perhaps the last such movement to take place successfully, the final enactment of an obsolete solution to social problems. On an individual scale, immigrants in contemporary days generally find themselves received by locals with resentment as competitors in the labour market of the country of their aspirations, and quickly sink to a place among the poor of that country. Nothing much has changed, over the centuries, except that we have evolved what might be called a philosophy of acceptance of poverty.

First, there is the question of different class perceptions of what poverty is, and how these are arrived at. There is the upper-class perception. There is the middle-class perception. And there is that of the poor themselves.

For the rich, any contingency that they themselves might sink into poverty is so remote that it need not enter their minds. They are also in the position of being *bountiful*; so that, curiously, while they may be genuinely concerned about the existence of the poor, poverty is also a source of self-esteem. Do not be shocked by this remark; without the philanthropy of wealth, the manner in which the world has dealt with, alleviated, poverty up till now could not have been maintained at all. But this over-spill of wealth is too sporadic, too personally dependent on what aspects of poverty, piece-meal, donors happen to favour, to be a solution.

I read recently that if an amount equal to the combined wealth of the ten richest individuals in the world could be made available annually, the problem of the world's 1.3 billion living in extreme poverty could be solved by the end of the century. And it seems one of the listed twenty richest (Ted Turner of CNN) has heard the message or taken the hint; and his remark that his one-billion dollar donation made available over ten years represents a mere nine months of his income gives credence to the incredible claim that the wealth of ten individuals is so great that it could solve the problem of poverty. Well, one cannot expect these individuals to give up their worldly goods *in toto* for the world, any more than any of us, I suspect, are prepared to sacrifice our—we consider—reasonable privileges entirely for those who have none. What is asked is for those who possess and control great wealth to look at the political and economic structures in their countries which have made that wealth possible and yet have created conditions that make philanthropy necessary—political and economic regimes that have failed to establish the means, in adequate pay for work, in education and training, in environment, by which people may provide for themselves in self-respect and dignity. That is the thinking that will face the facts of redistribution of the world's wealth.

The wealthy and powerful who control the consortiums and international companies, and the government agencies who plan with them, need to take responsible heed of the emphasis placed by the United Nations Development Programme on 'putting people at the centre of development'; on the concept of development enterprises as not only or even primarily advancing the credit balance of a country and providing X number of jobs, but as the instigation of a series of social consequences that will affect the implicated community in many ways. What may put pay in the pockets of the income poor this year may be off-set, over their lifetime, by destroying their environment. Development becomes a dangerous form of social engineering if it discounts the long-term effects on social cohesion. Profit and loss, in the book-keeping of the eradication of poverty, will be a calculation of how many people's daily lives can be entered, *in the long term*, on the credit column.

For the broad middle-class, which includes the skilled working-class in many countries, the possibility of descending to poverty is subliminally present. Their concept of poverty is tinged by fear, as well as by concern for those who suffer it: *there but for the grace of God go I*. Civil conflict, a change of government, inflation, a form of affirmative action whether on principle of colour, race, or simply replacement of older employees with the young—these contingencies threaten middle-class safety with its home ownership, its insurance policies and pension funds. All the things that poverty strips one of; all the safety-nets the poor do not have . . . Poverty is regarded as a blow of fate that just might come. Alternatively, in defensive rationalisation, whose fault is poverty, aside from national aleatory conditions? Perhaps, since the middle-class by and large is industrious and ambitious—and has the possibility of advancement in terms of money and status, having a base to start from which the poor have not—the middle-class often feels that it is lack of will, initiative, and commitment to work as they themselves do, that keeps the poor in that state.

The basic image of poverty is the man begging in the street; the conclusion: surely there's *something else* he could do? Unemployment is suspect as lack of ability; and well it may be in many developing countries where lack of skills makes people literally unemployable, unable to be active in sectors where employment would be available. But what has to be realized is how that lack comes about in the general disempowerment of poverty itself. To abolish the spectre of the man begging in the street, the woman huddled on her park-bench home, the children staring from a refugee camp, is first to make the effort to understand what factors create this disempowerment.

How do victims themselves perceive their poverty?

They live it; they know it best, beyond all outside concepts.

What, apart from the survival needs of food and shelter, do *they* feel they are most deprived of? Researchers moving among them have learned much that is often ignored, such as the perception of women that, as those who with their children suffer most, attention to their advancement should take more than a marginal 'special interest' place in transformation of the lives of the disadvantaged in general. Recent advice to the Hong Kong meeting of the World Bank and the IMF was that some fifteen thousand bankers, finance ministers, and representatives of development business attending 'might do well to re-dedicate themselves to slowing population growth through more attention to reproductive health, education for girls and employment for women'.

Consultation with how communities in poverty see them-

selves in relation to the ordinary fullness of life other communities take for granted is now recognized by research as integral to
harnessing the negatives of social resentment and passivity into
vital partnership for change. It is the fortunate world outside
dollar-a-day subsistence that needs to begin to see the impoverished as our necessary partners in world survival, partners to be
listened to in respect of the components of what a decent life is. It
is the privileged world that needs to come to the realization that
a 'decent life' cannot be truly lived by any of us while one-quarter
of the developing world's population exists in poverty.

If economic poverty began when some had surplus production and some did not, and nothing much has changed in principle, the second cause of poverty as a phenomenon of human
history is war, and nothing much has changed there, either.
Wars, social conflict, whether at international, national, or
inter-ethnic level, still produce hunger and homelessness, the
prime characteristics of poverty, and now, it seems, on a rolling
action scale, spreading as a deadly pandemic from one territory
to another. The eradication of poverty implies a hand-in-hand
relation with agencies of the non-violent resolution of conflict.
The peace-keeping, peace-promoting work of the United
Nations and other formations, fraught with difficulty, danger,
and frustration, and controversial as it is, must be seen as a vital
component of the decade's aim. The Secretary General of the
United Nations, Kofi Annan, has put the truth succinctly:
'Without peace development is not possible; without development peace is not possible.'

The violence of nature—flood, drought, and earthquake—is
another factor that has caused poverty since ancient times, and
that is something which is not within human capability to prevent, as wars are. But the violence perpetrated *by* humankind *on*
nature is increasingly one of the causes of poverty. The destruc-

tion of indigenous forests, the pollution of oceans, the leaching out of the land by indiscriminate use of chemicals; these take away from communities their livelihood. The leakage of nuclear waste makes water unpotable and, as the people of South-East Asia have so recently experienced, the hellish miasma from burned-out trees makes the very air unbreathable. The problem of poverty cannot be solved while the earth and its oceans that feed us are abused by ruthless government planning and blinkered human greed.

What are the moral perceptions of poverty?

These are governed by those looking on, looking in, so to speak, from the outside. 'Poor but honest': consider the dictum. Why do the rich never make the qualification, 'Rich but honest'? No-one has commented on moral attitudes in this context better than Bertolt Brecht. Here is his poem:

> *Food is the first thing. Morals follow on.*
> *So first make sure that those who now are starving*
> *Get proper helpings when we do the carving.*

Is for people to be honest when they are starving our measure of virtue, or is it a measure of our hypocrisy? Common crime, up to a certain level—economic white-collar crime is the prerogative of the wealthy—is a product of poverty and cannot be countered by punitive methods alone. Some of the funds that citizens, living in urban fear of muggings and robberies, want to see used, as the saying goes, to 'stamp out crime' with more police and bigger prisons, would have better effect diverted to the aim of stamping out poverty. No-one will be safe while punishment and pious moral dicta are handed out in place of food. The campaign against poverty is the best campaign against crime.

Finally, the definition of poverty does not end with material needs; the aim of its eradication will not be complete or perhaps even attainable without the world's attention to the deprivation of the mind: intellectual poverty. As food is the basic need of the starved body, literacy is the basic need of the starved mind. According to the United Nations Development Programme's *Human Development Report 1997*, in the past fifty years adult illiteracy in the world has been reduced to almost half. If it can be virtually ended by early next century, it will be a great force in the six-point global action plan provided by the Report, and not only because the ability to read and write is crucial to participation in development, the open sesame to the world of work, mental skills, and self-administration that is economic freedom. For to be illiterate or semi-literate is to be deprived of the illumination and pleasure of reading, of each individual's rightful share in an exploration of the world of ideas; it is to spend one's life imprisoned between the walls of one-dimensional experience.

Illiteracy cruelly stunts the human spirit both as a cause and as a result of the disempowerment we now dedicate a decade to bring to an end. We are here to discuss and pledge the means we know we have at our disposal; and I want to close with what I believe can be our text, for the day and the decade. It comes from William Blake.

Many conversed on these things as they labour'd at the furrow
Saying: 'It is better to prevent misery than to release from misery:
It is better to prevent error than to forgive the criminal.
Labour well the Minute Particulars, attend to the Little-ones,
And those who are in misery cannot remain so long
If we do but our duty: labour well the teeming Earth.'

—*Speech to the United Nations Development Programme, UN,*
Launch of 'Decade for Elimination of Poverty'
New York, October 17, 1997

The ceaseless adventure.

—Jawaharlal Nehru

THE WRITER'S IMAGINATION

AND THE IMAGINATION

OF THE STATE

⟶⊷⟵

The State has no imagination.

The State has no imagination because the State sees imagination as something that can be put into service.

The Writer is *put into service* by his imagination; he or she writes at its dictate.

The State is a collective intelligence. This is so whether it is arrived at by way of the Central Committee of the Party or whether it is the result of the long process of primaries and secondaries in a multi-party order. When the State projects a social vision—and it has no more concentrated unit of vision—it does so through the perceptions of planners, advisers, commissions, experts in this and that, ministers of this and that, constitutional lawyers, spokesmen, politicians. The formation of the State's vision is a process of *briefing*. Its product is social engineering.

The imagination can never be the product of a collective. It is the most concentrated of cerebral activities, the most exclusive, private, and individual. If there is a physiological explanation of it, I have never read one that matches the experience I know, and others do, as writers. Wicks along the way of the past—childhood or only yesterday, or even an hour ago, in the dark of time in which the Writer, unlike other people, is always comfortable, as a blind man feels along his darkness—these wicks are lit up one by one, and they are followed to caverns that were missed, where voices that did not complete what there was to say, sound on; places that have never been open to ordinary perception, or may be in time to come. For the Writer is connected with time; that is the imagination. The State is connected with history; the State has only *projection* in place of imagination. For the writer, those small lights fuse in a single vision and become the Cyclops eye. It is what that eye sees that no other does. Only the Writer him- or herself can focus that beam as a social product—poem, novel, or story. The inner eye of the State is one of those revolving balls made up of fragments of mirror which used to dominate old dance-halls. It winks all over the place, casting back upon all who pass under its surveillance whatever spotlight it chooses to illuminate itself with from without—turning faces timid with green, tense with violet, or happy with sunset-rose.

What kind of relation can there be between the imagination and the projection?

How do the Writer and the State get on?

We know that there have been examples of the imagination feeling at home within the projection; something close to what Lukács calls the duality of inwardness and outside world, overcome. This unity, then, becomes 'the divinatory-intuitive grasping of the unattained and therefore inexpressible meaning of life.' Time and history meet. And of course the philosophy of social order, from which the State selects for projection whatever serves the purpose of power in its particular circumstance (rebellious population, high unemployment, famine or plenty)—the philosophy of social order was first *imagined*, in the secular world, by writers, the writers of antiquity. It was from Plato's cavern of small lights that the shadows on the walls came out to try democracy, in the flesh. But what the State made of the ancients' visions of social order belongs to the realm of history and not imagination—extant in the forms of democracy that actually do exist in some countries of both East and West, and also in the kind of total travesty that exists in my own country, South Africa, where the State fantasizes (which is not at all the same thing as imagining) the projection of a 'democratic process' as a social order where the majority of the population has no vote.

But I believe that more often, in instances where time and history appear to have met, this has been, so to speak, before the event: the Writer's imagination has visualized an ordering of human lives that seems to be attainable by the projection of a State not yet created. The Risorgimento is one example. The Russian Revolution, in the vision of a Mayakovsky, another. And there are more. But once the State is established, the duality between Writer and State opens again. Why? I do not think the whole explanation is to be found in the stark fact that the ideals of a revolution are at best difficult to realize and at worst are betrayed, when the revolution itself succeeds. The Writer himself knows that the only revolution is the permanent one— not in the Trotskyite sense, but in the sense of the imagination, in which no understanding is ever completed, but must keep breaking up and re-forming in different combinations if it is to spread and meet the terrible questions of human existence. What alienates the Writer from the State is that the State—any State—is always certain it is right.

Brecht's imagination had an uneasy relationship with the projection of the State in East Germany; although his political beliefs were those he saw embodied in the idea of the State, the State's projection of the idea was not that of his imagination. His theory of epic theatre seemed orthodox enough (orthodoxy always belongs to the projection, of course); it was, in the words of Walter Benjamin, 'to discover the conditions of life'. That is what the Writer's imagination seeks to do everywhere; and as happened to Brecht, it is generally not exactly what the State would have from the Writer. The State wants from the Writer *reinforcement* of the type of consciousness it imposes on its citizens, not the discovery of the actual conditions of life beneath it, which may give the lie to it. The State wants this whether it is in the form of the pulp fiction where individualism is safely channelled as a monogram on a variety of consumer goods and the ideal of human achievement takes place not on earth at all, but is extraplanetary, or whether it is in the form of the incorruptible worker exposing the black marketeer, or whether—East or West—it is the retributory bad end of the spy who sells defence plans, his fate thus transforming the State's nuclear arms into the sacred sword of King Arthur.

Where the State's projection of social order allows it to do so, it often goes so far as to imprison the imagination, in the person of the Writer, or the banning of a book. Where the State says it welcomes and encourages assaults by the imagination on the State's projection, it invites the poet to dine at State House, and shores up if not the law, then something invoked as the traditional morality of the nation, against the breaches the high tide of the imagination has made in the consciousness of the State's subjects.

The imagination, freed in time, never forgets what the projection, bound in history, constantly rewrites and erases.

—*Address to PEN Congress*
New York, January 1986

WRITING AND BEING

⟶⚬⟵

In the beginning was the Word.

The Word was with God, signified God's Word, the word that was Creation. But over the centuries of human culture the word has taken on other meanings, secular as well as religious. To have the word has come to be synonymous with ultimate authority, with prestige, with awesome, sometimes dangerous persuasion, to have Prime Time, a TV talk show, to have the gift of the gab as well as that of speaking in tongues. The word flies through space, it is bounced from satellites, now nearer than it has ever been to the heaven from which it was believed to have come. But its most significant transformation occurred for me and my kind long ago, when it was first scratched on a stone tablet or traced on papyrus, when it materialized from sound to spectacle, from being heard to being read as a series of signs, and then a script; and travelled through time from parchment to Gutenberg. For this is the genesis story of the writer. It is the story that *wrote* her or him into being.

It was, strangely, a double process, creating at the same time both the writer and the very purpose of the writer as a mutation in the agency of human culture. It was both ontogenesis as the origin and development *of* an individual being, and the adaptation, in the nature of that individual, specifically *to* the exploration of ontogenesis, the origin and development of *the* individual being. For we writers are evolved for that task. Like the prisoner incarcerated with the jaguar in Borges' story 'The God's Script', who was trying to read, in a ray of light which fell only once a day, the meaning of being from the markings on the creature's pelt, we spend our lives attempting to interpret through the word the readings we take in the societies, the world of which we are part. It is in this sense, this inextricable, ineffable participation, that writing is always and at once an exploration of self and of the world; of individual and collective being.

Being here.

Humans, the only self-regarding animals, blessed or cursed with this torturing higher faculty, have always wanted to know why. And this is not just the great ontological question of why we are here at all, for which religions and philosophies have tried to answer conclusively for various peoples at various times, and science tentatively attempts dazzling bits of explanation we are perhaps going to become extinct, like dinosaurs, without having developed the necessary comprehension to understand as a whole. Since humans became self-regarding they have sought, as well, explanations for the common phenomena of procreation, death, the cycle of seasons, the earth, sea, wind and stars, sun and moon, plenty and disaster. With myth, the writer's ancestors, the oral story-tellers, began to feel out and formulate these mysteries, using the elements of daily life—observable reality—and the faculty of the imagination—the power of projection into the hidden—to make stories.

Roland Barthes asks, 'What is characteristic of myth?' And answers: 'To transform a meaning into form.' Myths are stories that mediate in this way between the known and unknown. Claude Lévi-Strauss wittily de-mythologizes myth as a genre between a fairy tale and a detective story. Being here; we don't know who-dun-it. But something satisfying, if not the answer, can be invented. Myth was the mystery plus the fantasy—gods, anthropomorphized animals and birds, chimeras, phantasmagorical creatures—that posits out of the imagination some sort of explanation for the mystery. Humans and their fellow creatures were the materiality of the story, but, as Nikos Kazantzakis once wrote, 'Art is the representation not of the body but of the forces which created the body.'

There are many proven explanations for natural phenomena now; and there are new questions of being arising out of some of the answers. For this reason, the genre of myth has never been entirely abandoned, although we are inclined to think of it as archaic. If it dwindled to the children's bedtime tale in some societies, in parts of the world protected by forests or deserts from international mega-culture, it has continued, alive, to offer art as a system of mediation between the individual and being. And it has made a whirling come-back out of Space, an Icarus in the avatar of Batman and his kind, who never fall into the ocean of failure to deal with the gravity forces of life.

These new myths, however, do not seek so much to enlighten and provide some sort of answers as to distract, to provide a fantasy escape route for people who no longer want to face even the hazard of answers to the terrors of their existence. (Perhaps it is the positive knowledge that humans now possess the means to destroy their whole planet, the fear that they have in this way themselves become the gods, dreadfully charged with their own continued existence, that has made comic-book and movie-myth escapism.) The forces of being remain. They are what the writer, as distinct from the contemporary popular myth-maker, still engages today, as myth in its ancient form attempted to do.

How writers have approached this engagement and continue to experiment with it has been and is, perhaps more than ever, the study of literary scholars. The writer in relation to the nature of perceivable reality and what is beyond—imperceivable reality—is the basis for all these studies, no matter what resulting concepts are labelled, and no matter in what categorized microfiles writers are stowed away for the annals of literary historiography. Reality is constructed out of many elements and entities, seen and unseen, expressed and left unexpressed for breathing-space in the mind. Yet from what is regarded as old-hat psychological analysis to structuralism and post-structuralism, modernism and post-modernism, all literary studies are aimed at the same end: to pin down to a consistency (and what is consistency if not the principle hidden within the riddle?); to make definitive through methodology the writer's grasp at the forces of being. But life is aleatory in itself; being is constantly pulled and shaped this way and that by circumstances and different levels of consciousness. There is no pure state of being, and it follows that there is no pure text, 'real' text, totally incorporating the aleatory. It surely cannot be reached by any critical methodology, however interesting the attempt. To deconstruct a text is in a way a contradiction, since to deconstruct it is to make another construction out of the pieces, as Roland Barthes does so fascinatingly, and admits to, in his linguistic and semantical dissection of Balzac's story 'Sarrasine'. So the literary scholars end up being some kind of story-teller, too.

Perhaps there is no other way of reaching some understanding of being than through art? Writers themselves don't analyze what they do; to analyze would be to look down while crossing a canyon on a tightrope. To say this is not to mystify the process of writing but to make an image out of the intense inner concentration the writer must have to cross the chasms of the aleatory and make them the word's own, as an explorer plants a flag. Yeats's inner 'lonely impulse of delight' in the pilot's solitary flight, and his 'terrible beauty' born of mass uprising, both opposed and conjoined; E. M. Forster's modest 'only connect'; Joyce's chosen, wily 'silence, cunning and exile'; more contemporary, Gabriel García Márquez's labyrinth in which power over others, in the person of Simon Bolivar, is led to the thrall of the only unassailable power, death—these are some examples of the writer's endlessly varied ways of approaching the state of being through the word. Any writer of any worth at all hopes to play only a pocket-torch of light—and rarely, through genius, a sudden flambeau—into the bloody yet beautiful labyrinth of human experience, of being.

Anthony Burgess once gave a summary definition of literature as 'the aesthetic exploration of the word'. I would say that writing only begins there, for the exploration of much beyond, which nevertheless only aesthetic means can express.

How does the writer become one, having been given the word? I do not know if my own beginnings have any particular interest. No doubt they have much in common with those of others, have been described too often.

For myself, I have said that nothing factual that I write or say will be as truthful as my fiction. The life, the opinions, are not the work, for it is in the tension between standing apart and being involved that the imagination transforms both. Let me give some minimal account of myself. I am what I suppose would be called a natural writer. I did not make any decision to become one. I did not, at the beginning, expect to earn a living by being read. I wrote as a child out of the joy of apprehending life through my senses—the look and scent and feel of things; and soon out of the emotions that puzzled me or raged within me and which took form, found some enlightenment, solace, and delight, shaped in the written word. There is a little Kafka parable that goes like this: 'I have three dogs: Hold-him, Seize-him, and Nevermore. Hold-him and Seize-him are ordinary little Schipperkes and nobody would notice them if they were alone. But there is Nevermore, too. Nevermore is a mongrel Great Dane and has an appearance that centuries of the most careful breeding could never have produced. Nevermore is a gypsy.' In the small South African gold-mining town where I was growing up I was Nevermore the mongrel (although I could scarcely have been described as a Great Dane . . .) in whom the accepted characteristics of the townspeople could not be traced. I was the Gypsy, tinkering with words second-hand, mending my own efforts at writing by learning from what I read. For my school was the local library. Proust, Chekhov, and Dostoevsky, to name only a few to whom I owe my existence as a writer, were my professors. In that period of my life, yes, I *was* evidence of the theory that books are made out of other books . . . But I did not remain so for long, nor do I believe any potential writer could.

With adolescence comes the first reaching out to otherness through the drive of sexuality. For most children, from then on the faculty of the imagination, manifest in play, is lost in the focus on day-dreams of desire and love, but for those who are going to be artists of one kind or another the first life-crisis after that of birth does something else in addition: the imagination gains range and extends by the subjective flex of new and turbulent emotions. There are new perceptions. The writer begins to be able to enter into other lives. The process of standing apart and being involved has come.

Unknowingly, I had been addressing myself on the subject of being, whether, as in my first stories, there was a child's contemplation of death and murder in the necessity to finish off, with a death blow, a dove mauled by a cat, or whether there was wondering dismay and early consciousness of racism that came of my walk to school, when on the way I passed store-keepers, themselves East European immigrants kept lowest in the ranks of the Anglo-Colonial social scale for whites in the mining town, roughly abusing those whom colonial society ranked lowest of all, discounted as less than human—the black miners who were the store's customers. Only many years later was I to realize that if I had been a child in that category—black—I might not have become a writer at all, since the library that made this possible for me was not open to any black child. For my formal schooling was sketchy, at best.

To address oneself to others begins a writer's next stage of development. To publish: to publish to anyone who would read what I wrote. That was my natural, innocent assumption of what publication meant, and it has not changed; that is what it means to me today, in spite of my awareness that most people refuse to believe that a writer does not have a particular audience in mind; and my other awareness: of the temptations, conscious and unconscious, which lure the writer into keeping a corner of the eye on who will take offense, who will approve what is on the page—a temptation that, like Orpheus' straying glance, will lead the writer back into the Shades of a destroyed talent.

The alternative is not the malediction of the ivory tower,

another destroyer of creativity. Borges once said he wrote for his friends and to pass the time. I think this was an irritated flippant response to the crass question—often an accusation—'For whom do you write?' just as Sartre's admonition that there are times when a writer should cease to write, and act upon being only in another way, was given in the frustration of an unresolved conflict between distress at injustice in the world and the knowledge that what he knew how to do best was write. Both Borges and Sartre, from their totally different extremes of denying literature a social purpose, were certainly perfectly aware that it has its implicit and unalterable social role in exploring the state of being, from which all other roles, personal among friends, public at the protest demonstration, derive. Borges was not writing for his friends, for he published and we all have received the bounty of his work. Sartre did not stop writing, although he stood at the barricades in 1968.

The question of for whom do we write nevertheless plagues the writer, a tin can attached to the tail of every work published. Principally it jangles the inference of tendentiousness as praise or denigration. In this context, Camus dealt with the question best. He said that he liked individuals who take sides more than literatures that do. 'One either serves the whole of man or one does not serve him at all. And if man needs bread and justice, and if what has to be done must be done to serve this need, he also needs pure beauty, which is the bread of his heart.' So Camus called for 'Courage in one's life and talent in one's work.' And García Márquez redefined *tendenz* fiction thus: 'The best way a writer can serve a revolution is to write as well as he can.'

I believe that these two statements might be the credo for all of us who write. They do not resolve the conflicts that have come, and will continue to come, to contemporary writers. But

they state plainly an honest possibility of doing so, they turn
the face of the writer squarely to her and his existence, the reason to be, as a writer, and the reason to be, as a responsible
human, acting, like any other, within a social context.

Being here: in a particular time and place. That is the existential position with particular implications for literature. Czeslaw
Milosz once wrote the cry: 'What is poetry which does not serve
nations or people?' and Brecht wrote of a time when 'to speak of
trees is almost a crime'. Many of us have had such despairing
thoughts while living and writing through such times, in such
places, and Sartre's solution makes no sense in a world where
writers were—and still are—censored and forbidden to write,
where, far from abandoning the word, lives were and are at risk
in smuggling it, on scraps of paper, out of prisons. The state of
being whose ontogenesis we explore has overwhelmingly
included such experiences. Our approaches, in Nikos Kazantzakis's words, have to 'make the decision which harmonizes with
the fearsome rhythm of our time.'

Some of us have seen our books lie for years unread in our
own countries, banned, and we have gone on writing. Many
writers have been imprisoned. Looking at Africa alone—
Soyinka, Ngugi wa Thiong'o, Jack Mapanje, in their countries,
and in my own country, South Africa, Jeremy Cronin, Mongane
Wally Serote, Breyten Breytenbach, Dennis Brutus, Jaki Seroke:
all these went to prison for the courage shown in their lives, and
have continued to take the right, as poets, to speak of trees.
Many of the greats, from Thomas Mann to Chinua Achebe, cast
out by political conflict and oppression in different countries,
have endured the trauma of exile, from which some never
recover as writers, and some do not survive at all. I think of the

South Africans, Can Themba, Alex La Guma, Nat Nakasa, Todd Matshikiza. And some writers, over half a century, from Joseph Roth to Milan Kundera, have had to publish new works first in the word that is not their own, a foreign language.

Then in 1988 the fearsome rhythm of our time quickened in an unprecedented frenzy to which the writer was summoned to submit the word. In the broad span of modern times since the Enlightenment writers have suffered opprobrium, bannings, and even exile for other than political reasons. Flaubert dragged into court for indecency, over *Madame Bovary*, Strindberg arraigned for blasphemy, over *Marrying*, Lawrence's *Lady Chatterley's Lover* banned—there have been many examples of so-called offense against hypocritical bourgeois mores, just as there have been of treason against political dictatorships. But in a period when it would be unheard of for countries such as France, Sweden, and Britain to bring such charges against freedom of expression, there has risen a force that takes its appalling authority from something far more widespread than social mores, and far more powerful than the power of any single political regime. The edict of a world religion has sentenced a writer to death.

For more than four years, now, wherever he is hidden, wherever he might go, Salman Rushdie has existed under the Muslim pronouncement upon him of the *fatwa*. Every morning when this writer sits down to write, he does not know if he will live through the day; he does not know whether the page will ever be filled. Salman Rushdie happens to be a brilliant writer, and the novel for which he is being pilloried, *The Satanic Verses*, is an innovative exploration of one of the most intense experiences of being in our era, the individual personality in transition between two cultures brought together in a post-colonial world. All is re-examined through the refraction of the imagination; the meaning of sexual and filial love, the rituals of social acceptance, the meaning of a formative religious faith for individuals removed

from its subjectivity by circumstance opposing different systems
of belief, religious and secular, in a different context of living.
His novel is a true mythology. But although he has done for the
post-colonial consciousness what Günter Grass did for the post-
Nazi one with *The Tin Drum* and *Dog Years*, perhaps even has
tried to approach what Beckett did for our existential anguish in
Waiting for Godot, the level of his achievement should not matter. Even if he were a mediocre writer, his situation is the terrible concern of every fellow writer for, apart from his personal
plight, what implications, what new threat against the carrier of
the word does it bring? It should be the concern of individuals
and, above all, of governments and human rights organizations
all over the world. With dictatorships apparently vanquished,
this murderous new dictate invoking the power of international
terrorism in the name of a great and respected religion should
and can be dealt with only by democratic governments and the
United Nations, as an offense against humanity.

To return from the horrific singular threat to those that have been
general for writers of this century now in its final, summing-up
decade. In repressive regimes anywhere, whether in what was the
Soviet bloc, Latin America, Africa, China—most imprisoned
writers have been shut away for their activities as citizens striving
for liberation against the oppression of the general society to
which they belong. Others have been condemned by repressive
regimes for serving society by writing as well as they can; for this
aesthetic venture of ours becomes subversive when the shameful
secrets of our times are explored profoundly, with the artist's
rebellious integrity to the state-of-being manifest in life around
her or him; then the writer's themes and characters inevitably are
formed by the pressures and distortions of that society as the life
of the fisherman is determined by the power of the sea.

There is a paradox. In retaining this integrity, the writer sometimes must risk both the state's indictment of treason and the liberation forces' complaint of lack of blind commitment. As a human being, no writer can stoop to the lie of Manichaean 'balance'. The devil always has lead in his shoes, when placed on his side of the scale. Yet, to paraphrase coarsely García Márquez's dictum given by him both as a writer and as a fighter for justice, the writer must take the right to explore, warts and all, both the enemy and the beloved comrade-in-arms, since only a try for the truth makes sense of being, only a try for the truth edges towards justice just ahead of Yeats's beast slouching to be born.

The writer is of service to humankind only insofar as the writer uses the word even against his or her own loyalties, trusts the state of being, as it is revealed, to hold somewhere in its complexity filaments of the cord of truth, able to be bound together, here and there, in art; trusts the state of being to yield somewhere fragmentary phrases of truth, which is the final word of words, never changed by our stumbling efforts to spell it out and write it down, never changed by lies, by semantic sophistry, by the dirtying of the word for the purposes of racism, sexism, prejudice, domination, the glorification of destruction, the curses and the praise-songs.

—*Nobel Prize Lecture, 1991*

LIVING ON

A FRONTIERLESS LAND:

CULTURAL GLOBALIZATION

—⟫●⟨—

rocess noun, GLOCALIZATION. Formed by telescoping *global* and *local* to make a blend; the idea is modeled on Japanese *dochakuka* (derived from *dochaku*, "living on one's own land"), originally the agricultural principle of adapting one's farming techniques to local conditions, but also adopted in Japanese business . . . for *global localization*, a global outlook adapted to local conditions. The idea of going for the world market (global marketing) was a feature of business thinking in the early Eighties. By the late Eighties and early Nineties, Western companies had observed the success of Japanese firms in doing this while at the same time exploiting local conditions as well.'—*Oxford Dictionary of New Words*, 1991

That is the etymology of a word that is not yet recorded in that dictionary, *Globalization*. There is always something to learn from the way a term such as this one, now widely and unthinkingly used by us all, has been derived. Then we shall at least know, by its origins, exactly what we're talking about. The term has emerged out of need for the expression of political, economic, social, and cultural changes. It's an omnibus term, of course, not only carrying its variety of passenger interest, but travelling to and through different terrains. The best-known and accepted of these is, indeed, that for which the term was coined, while elaborating on its original limitations in Japanese understanding: the expansion of trade over the oceans and air-space, beyond traditional alliances which were restricted by old political spheres of influence, particularly in the era of colonialism, and by the barriers of the Cold War. Now there are new formations hiding behind the acronyms of new groupings of countries on the world terrain of trade, but at the same time other barriers, important ones, are being breached. One has only to glance round at the occupants of business-class seats in aircraft to see the flying caravan (I change metaphors) of government trade missions, industrialists and merchants, busy at their laptops in preparation for presentations that will vend—more valuable than spices ever were—minerals and commodities, industrial, mining, and communications plant, and—yes—arms, to the world-wide oases of buyers, who in turn will have something to sell: resources natural and manufactured which the traders lack back home.

Does the globalization of culture follow the same process?

On the principle of opening up the bounty of our world, ill-distributed as it has been by both nature and humans, it does. Both are gathered under the rubric of human development which is now understood as not achievable in isolation by any one country or even grouping of countries—a down-to-earth acceptance that we cannot come closer than this to the idealistic (and ideological) concept of one world which some of us are old enough to remember nostalgically. But the great difference is that culture is a 'trade' foremost in intangibles, not materials and money, and it is, paradoxically, both its power and its weakness that it is only partially dependent on the exchange of money in order to operate.

In its essence, much of real culture, as opposed to the exploitation of culture as a billboard, TV-slot public relations commodity, has no market value. The exceptions, anyone will be quick to point out, are the popular music groups and individual musicians, arising in their home countries genuinely from the people's culture rather than any elite, who are celebrated and highly paid while at the same time making the musical heritage of their own countries known and appreciated, all over the world. But writers who come from, let us say, Canada, Norway, Cuba, Egypt, to a poetry conference in Australia, dancers who come from Japan, India, the U.S.A., Spain, to a workshop in Ghana—their 'rate of exchange' is the expansion of ideas, the possibilities of their art, as coming from the life and spirit of the Other, the unknown country and society. No material benefit is involved beyond the staples of an airfare, food, and lodging . . . The concept of selling and buying as a principle of globalization does not apply. The ethic of mutual enrichment without consideration of material profit is that of *cultural* globalization; by the very nature of *trade* globalization of the world's material resources, this ethic is secondary to it.

Once one moves into the dimension of ethics, many questions present themselves. First, one must examine what the aim of globalization of culture is, or, to be less didactic, could be. Is it, in the attempt to heal the peoples of the world in their wounding divisions, the manifestations of xenophobia that underlie conflict, an aim of emphasizing the unity, the *oneness* of cultural expression? Therefore a conformity, even if of the highest order? A tactic to avoid value judgments of which is the highest art form among those achieved nationally, judgments influenced by the nature of what is regarded as culture in the various countries making such judgments? Or is the aim to *value the differences*, bring them into play across aesthetic frontiers and thus disprove the long-held sovereignty of national and political divisions over the development of human potential?

Most of us would agree the aim is the latter. Yet each answer brings another question; immediately, this is the question of language, since language is the means of many cultural activities corollary to the great one of literature itself. It is vital to that field of mixed media, the image and the spoken word, in the theatre and the theatre's international extension, TV drama. Intellectual debate depends on language, although the exchange of ideas and insight comes without need of words in the revelation of paintings and music. Care has to be taken, however, that one or two of the short list of self-styled world languages do not become decisive in our reach for globalization of culture. This could be a subconscious lapse into the very state the concept of freeing culture seeks to end; a value decision that high culture, true culture, resides within those international 'families' allied by language affiliations (Romance languages, for example), shared frontiers decided after old wars, political alignments and realignments, ideological loyalties. The short list can't be justified on account of number of speakers of a language, since vastly-spoken Chinese and Arabic don't feature on it. Of course they don't; and why? Because it is out of the old conditioning of Western culture, 'the formidable structure of cultural domination' Edward Said cites, that much of the drive towards cultural globalization, creativity freed to roam and procreate, has come; old habits engender autocratic attitudes that die hard!

As one of the speakers and writers of one of those 'world languages', am I advocating that globalization means everyone must learn Chinese in order for this to be realized? Hardly a feasible condition, even if desirable. No doubt the Chinese, along with the Arabs, the Japanese, and others will have to learn English, French, German, and Spanish, as they are already doing, perforce, in pursuit of the *other* form of globalization, trade and technology. As for the peoples of Africa, they are already long accustomed to the imperative of learning the languages of the West, depending on under which colonial rule they have lived. But if cultural globalization is to be more than another failed One World, it must be conceived genuinely broadly in active cognition that there should be no hierarchy of languages directing it.

What practical steps can be suggested to tackling with more than such statements this huge problem of words?

Since literature is the heavy-duty vehicle of the Word, carrying a large freight of culture, cross-translation of the literature of the languages of the world is an important part of the answer. This requires co-operation between publishing houses world-wide, in reciprocal publication of works of fiction, poetry, drama, and general prose beyond the category of journalism—this last reaches most peoples and languages through the international networks of translation in newspapers and on television newscasts. The Departments of Culture in governments have a neglected responsibility, in terms of the extension of their *own* countries' cultures, to subsidize such publication, and, indeed, it must be seen not as some luxury subvention, but recognized also by the Departments of Foreign Affairs as a logical part of their function in developing peaceful, fruitful, and progressive relations with other countries: allocation from Foreign Affairs' budgets should be mandatory.

Exchange visits of writers, artists, dramatists, film-makers, composers, musicians, dancers—every means of expression of the arts—have been growing, but although the embassies of many countries are helpful in funding these on behalf of their nationals, many more exchanges are needed to give practitioners of the arts the chance to enrich one another's ability and spread creative variety and innovation. Diseases, alas, are pandemic; in our world on the eve of the new millennium, art is not. Again, subvention from governments and business—the brothers and sisters from *their* side of the globalization process, international trade—is imperative if cultural globalization is to be achievable.

How, in national specificity, does each country go about moving beyond itself to procreate a culture that will benefit self and others? In some cases, the effort must begin at home on the country's own continent. If I single out my own country, South Africa, it is not only as personal special interest, but because South Africa was *the* example, the epitome of cultural isolation, suffered until apartheid was defeated by the liberation movements and a government of national unity, led by the African National Congress, was formed in 1994. Economic sanctions and cultural boycotts, which were stoically endured as necessary to end the apartheid regime, meant for the cultural community that we were cut off not only from Europe and the Americas but also from the rest of the continent to which we belong, even countries of some of our closest neighbours. Our first action, therefore, has been the fulfilling one of inviting our African counterparts around us to bring their literary culture to our country, and to take up return visits to theirs.

Isolation from our own continent predated, in fact, that of the apartheid era. Preceding it, the cultural domination of the North–South axis was imposed by colonisation-cum-Europeanisation (the latter persisted even when South Africa was no longer a British colony, but the white-ruled independent Union of South Africa); this meant that cultural connections were with Europe and North America almost exclusively: their literature, their theatre, their music and plastic arts. The arts of the continent to which we belonged were relegated to the anthropology departments of universities.

From our new establishment of connection with the *creativity of our African selfhood* we also have begun to move out of the restriction of North–South culture, invaluable though it remains in the cultural collective, to profit from the untapped South–South opportunities and—above all—affinities, that Eurocentric colonial attitudes ignored and denied us. South African writers and artists are exchanging working visits with their counterparts in

Brazil, Argentina, Uruguay, Chile, and Cuba, among other countries on the side of the world that matches our own, not least in the presence of the descendants of Africans who, enslaved, yet took eternal elements of African culture with them.

This South–South initiative, now only in its beginnings, is surely something that Europe and North America could pursue along with us, rather more vigorously than it appears they do, set within their cultural parameters, for even the riches of Western culture are limiting, in the context of a global culture.

Globalization is a circular, not a linear concept; the very root of the word implies this shape of wholeness, at once a setting forth and receiving in one continuous movement. And in confirmation of this, I find myself returned to what perhaps should have been my beginning: what do we mean by 'culture'? I have assumed the mandate of my subject was culture-as-the-arts, inclusive of the crafts. But culture has many definitions, constantly argued. For some people, it would include, for example, the cultural implications of food—I think of Claude Lévi-Strauss's splendid exegesis, *The Raw and the Cooked*. Mores and manners, too, are acculturated; above all, technology invades—shades into?—culture of the arts when, as now, people engage in cultural exchange of a kind, in the contradictory isolation, alone with a screen, through texts and graphics conjured up on the Internet. There is even a lyricism of international Internet jargon—its basic procedure is known by the poetic verbal imagery 'surfing the Net'. Is this a globalization of poetry on a scale previously unimaginable, or a sign of the global subsumption of the arts in the unquestionable, already achieved globalization of electronics?

When we speak of the globalization of culture, North, South, East, West, we have still to decide what these other parameters of it are. Only then can we make reality of culture 'living on its own land': the frontierless territory of creativity.

OUR CENTURY

O ur century.

Our defining claim, for I do not think it likely there is anyone here among us who dates from the nineteenth century? And if there should be some ancient patriarch or matriarch, then that venerable survivor certainly will have lived the major part of the human span in the twentieth.

My century. I share it with all: I was born in the first quarter and here I am, still living, in this, the final decade.

Even for those who are young and whose lives will move over to maturity in the twenty-first century, the turn of a century is the striking of a special midnight; when the first two digits of the date change, it is not the familiar movement of a clock's hands shifting to a new day, it is the toll that ends an era, it is an anniversary in recorded history, a birthday for humanity.

Whether this means that the human race is ageing, or whether it means that it is growing up, we—who have invented the measure of time but cannot, in our fragile container of flesh, conceive of time lived as millennia—cannot say.

A hundred years is the largest unit we can grasp, in terms of human life. After a hundred years, quantification begins again; it is not without significance that life is renewed in the Sleeping Beauty's family castle after one hundred years. The turn of a century is the prince's kiss of Time. On the first morning of 2000, the world will be awakened to a new calendar, perhaps a new life.

What has ours, our life in the twentieth century been?

I am not an historian and I hope I shall not disappoint too much those who expect a scholarly and comprehensive treatise on twentieth-century history, not a date or a treaty missing. On the other hand, I may also reassure those who dread such a treatise that they are not going to be subject to it.

Of course, there are consequences of my grave limitations.

Many wars, many changes of frontier, many schismatic ideologies, many important thinkers, will be missing. Significance, in human consciousness, is consistent only for real historians. Many scientific discoveries will be ignored, while others are seen as crucial to certain aspects of our life. As a child of this century who has experienced personally at least part of its radical momentum and sought to explore and understand more in the experience and consciousness of others, the conception of our century I gather together now is subjective. The curve of our existence is being followed by my eye. I hope this is subjectivity not in the sense of confined to myself, but rather to that naturally shared with many others shaped by the same period.

Living in the twentieth century, we cannot look upon it from the pretence of another perspective; nor should we try to if we are to discover what only we, if secretly, suppressedly, know best: the truth about ourselves, our time.

Has it been the worst of times?

Has it been the best of times?

Or should we combine the two extremes in the Dickensian fashion: 'It was the best of times, it was the worst of times'?

At once there arises from a flash brighter than a thousand suns the mushroom cloud that hangs over our century.

Exploded almost exactly at the half-century, the atomic bombs that destroyed Hiroshima and Nagasaki rise as unsurpassed evil done, even in this century where more human beings have been killed or allowed to die of starvation and disease, by human decision, than ever before in history; where the Nazi Holocaust, fifty years on, has become household words of horror as 'ethnic cleansing' in the Balkans and in Africa.

Unsurpassed evil because not only does an atom bomb kill and maim, it curses the children of survivors, the unborn, with monstrous physical and mental defects.

Unsurpassed evil laid at our door, certainly, because foremost of the 'firsts' our century can claim is that for the first time man (and I use the male gender accurately, specifically) invented a power of destruction which surpasses any natural catastrophe—the power of earthquake, volcano eruption, flood. Thus the final conquest of nature, an aim pursued with the object of human benefit since the invention of agriculture in the Stone Age, has been achieved in our discovery of how to wipe ourselves out more quickly and efficiently than any force of nature. The demonic vow of our century seems to come from Virgil: 'If I cannot move Heaven, I will stir up Hell.'

Six million Jews were gased or starved to death in a systematic process. It defined unspeakable years in our century. President Truman's ordering of the destruction of Hiroshima and Nagasaki brought 'the defining moments of terror' in our century. Kenzaburo Oe, Japanese Nobel Laureate in Literature, compiled an anthology of stories by Japanese writers of which he says he has come to realize these 'are not merely literary expressions, composed by looking back at the past, of what happened at Hiroshima and Nagasaki in the summer of 1945. They are also highly significant vehicles for thinking about the contemporary world . . . because civilisation is headed either towards extinction or towards salvation from that fate, we inescapably face an unknowable future.'

Japan re-created itself, up from the twisted wreckage, as an economic success rivalling that of the country that devastated it, and Japan has accepted as part of normal public health services the care of people skinned by atomic burns and children born with missing limbs or faculties, and the long-term effects of radiation sickness.

The signing of a Nuclear Non-Proliferation Treaty is brokered among nations, and the threat of an atomic war, which for forty years depended on the press of a button in the Pentagon or the Kremlin, is complacently half-forgotten since one protagonist in a Cold War is *hors de combat*. But the French, on the fiftieth anniversary of the atomic bombings of Japan, tried out their nuclear capacity, as if these loathsome apocalyptic weapons were now old toys a safe world can play with reminiscently.

T. S. Eliot's prediction was that we would end with a whimper; ours is that we could go out with a bang. The mushroom cloud still hangs over us; will it be there as a bequest to the new century?

The strange relation between the forces of Good and Evil has been part of the mystery of human existence since we evolved as the only self-regarding creatures in the animal world. The relation has been codified through successive civilisations in mythical, religious, or secular philosophical terms, without arriving at an explanation that could satisfy all three.

In our century, with its great leaps into what was formerly beyond human experience, the relation surely has become profoundly relevant and more inexplicable than ever.

Our time has produced genius beyond imagining: Albert Einstein was such a one. This shaggy, gentle scientist, a good man exiled from his home country by a force of evil, Nazism, deciphered one of the greatest secrets of nature, split the atom. What was intended to enrich humankind with an extension of knowledge of its cosmic existence, as a consequence produced out of Good the malediction of our time: atomic capability, in whomsoever's hands it remains or passes to.

I am not proposing, nor would it be acceptable to me personally, the equation of Manichaeism. A God or gods on one side inevitably implying a balance with the Devil or devils on the other—that's too easy to serve as an explanation for all the nuances of moral complication we know around and within us. What is more puzzling and far more troubling is what appears to be a kind of symbiosis. Good and Evil pass from one into the other through some transparency we, bewilderedly, cannot fathom. Or they share ganglia in systemic energy we cannot separate; or which perhaps cannot be separated. We try to apply moral precepts to processes that function according to *quite other laws*, laws in which this human construct of ours, morality, does not exist at all.

A sober contemplation for an age characterised by revolutionary scientific discovery.

If we turn away slightly, at an angle, from the absolutes of opposing Good and Evil as we see them, and must see them while human values are to survive, we come to the lower level—of paradox.

We have made spectacular advances in discoveries that have made life more bearable for some and more pleasurable for others.

We have eliminated many epidemics and alleviated much pain with new drugs; we have raised the dead in a real sense, by taking the vital organs from the dead and planting them to function again in the living; a symphony may be heard by means of a small disc thin as a crêpe Suzette; aircraft has revolutionized the possibility of physical presence. The bundle of telecommunications—computer, fax, e-mail, cellular phone—has speeded up communication by the spoken and written word; we have built towers that penetrate the clouds, we have lifted the burden of manual workers and housewives by machines programmed to do onerous tasks; with other machines we have brought music and moving images into every house.

We are the century whose inhabitants passed in one lifetime from riding in a horse-drawn cart or catching a train to as unremarkably boarding a plane; the first to look upon the world from 10,000 metres, from the angels' realm, the sphere of the heavens. Most of us have enjoyed some of these embellishments of life.

The Italian Futurist painters in the early decades of our age depicted in their imagination this world, which is now ours, as a world of sleek cars whirling unhampered through streets, planes buzzing like happy bees gathering the nectar of a new age between sky-scrapers and rainbows in a radiantly clear sky. Their paintings look to us now like the work of a Grandma Moses of industrialization; yet we shared this innocent ignorance of pollution, lacked with these artists the true vision of the future, which was that we would begin to choke on our technological progress, suffocate in our cities in our own foul breath of fumes and carcinogenic vapours. We have achieved much, but we have not always stayed at the controls of purpose.

It is also intriguing to observe in ourselves how technology has intervened in the intangible, telescoping our emotions. Those antipodean states, dread and anticipation, have been out-dated. Our nineteenth-century forefathers and mothers would have to wait weeks or months for any exchange of true minds by post— the telegram was too perfunctory and public to serve for anything more intimate than news of death or wars.

In our century, the ordeal of dread is banished by instant full communication from anywhere to anywhere. And as for anticipation, that becomes instant gratification. So, not for the first or last time, the advances of technology contradict theories of human satisfaction expounded by the savants of that other kind of advance in knowledge that has dramatically distinguished our century, psychoanalysis. Apart from its purely sexual application, Freud's deferred gratification as a refinement of emotional experience does not compare, for us, with the immediate joy of hearing a lover's voice, or getting a friend's reply to a letter, at once, by e-mail. Ours is the Age of Impatience that does not look forward to something: wants it now. Expects to have it, and gets it, so far as technology can provide it.

Even adventurism has been transformed by technology. The intrepid of the Euro-Russo-American world walk on the moon and dangle in space instead of 'discovering' jungles and rivers the indigenous inhabitants have known as home since their personal creation myths explained their presence there. The new adventurers *actually experience*, by weightlessness, *extinction while still alive*, become phantoms whose feet do not touch earth. They are the successors to the angels we, alas, no longer believe in because we have probed outer space and found no heaven.

What has been the impact on the arts, in our century of unprecedented technological development?

Perhaps only the twenty-first century will be able to assess this; we are too involved. We hear too much, we are brain-washed and conditioned by the areas of culture that have been made over by technology, or we struggle too obstinately against what surely has brought some benefits.

Technology is the means by which one of the positive consequences of the revolutions of the century—bloody or peaceful, failed or surviving—the determination to break open the elitism of the arts, has been made practical. It has brought into practice the challenge to the middle-class idea that you have to rise from the working or peasant class, somehow exceed your supposed natural disadvantages, become gentrified, to deserve and be able to enjoy the arts. This idea—of the upper classes, of course—always failed to note that the contemporary working and peasant classes had artistic values and activities of their own from which the middle-class were cut off by their self-imposed limitations in recognizing no creativity other than that of their own kind.

As for the great art of the past of what were known as indigenous (read 'inferior') peoples, from Mayan temples to Egyptian tombs—while that was greatly admired and even acknowledged as a useful inspiration for new forms (think of Picasso's debt to West African sculpture), it had long been considered, even by the intellectual elite within the countries to which this great art belonged as national heritage, as something that was not within the range of aesthetic appreciation by the ordinary people, although in some instances it still served the purpose of religious worship. From the era of troupes of actors and art exhibitions travelling through the villages of Russia after the October Revolution, to this decade of the nineties when villages and even squatter camps in Africa, in India, the Middle East, have transistor radios, and television sets are run on car batteries, culture in its most easily assimilable form—entertainment sugaring information—has been democratized. There has been a redistribution of intellectual privilege through technology.

Of course there have been changes in the concept of culture; mass usage inevitably makes transformations.

Pop, reggae, rock, rap concerts gather huge crowds, all over the world, which vastly exceed any audience that Bach and Mozart have brought together. This music is the only example I can cite which justifies the current wishful fantasy of the world as the 'global village'—through radio, cassette and disc, democratic communication of the arts succeeds in unifying peoples, at least in vociferous, sometimes ecstatic appreciation,

across bitterly-contested frontiers. Those who see the forms of
the music itself, the nature of popular appreciation it arouses, as
a limitation within the democratization of the arts, a deprivation chosen *for themselves* by the masses, at least must admit that
discs, and broadcasts which may be heard on the humblest
of radios, can provide glorious music for people who never have
had the money or opportunity to attend a live concert or opera.
And by the same means a recognition and appreciation of
the musical forms of the East and of Africa, from the classical
ragas of Ravi Shankar to the jazz of South Africa's *kwela* and
mbaqanga, have spread internationally.

Yet the overwhelming cultural transformation has been
brought about by television.

Television has altered human perception. It has changed the
means of knowing; of receiving the world.

Of the five senses, sight now outstrips all others; watching is
the most important form of comprehension. Although television speaks, it is its endless stream of images, out of which the
child, the youth, even mature and old who have had considerable direct experience of life, construct reality. There used to be
the concept of someone being 'lost' in a book, the fictional characters more live than those around the reader; this alternative
construct of environment, human personality, situation, made
out of the printed word, was flimsy in comparison with the
visual other world renewed in palimpsest after palimpsest, day
after day, night after night, for millions the last vision before
sleep and the first wakened to in the morning.

The influence of this *vicariously visual* experience on painting
begins to overtake some of the other movements which have
transformed art in our century, in which John Willet has noted
'a plea for the revival of the imagination, based on the Unconscious as revealed by psychoanalysis, together with a new
emphasis on magic, accident, irrationality, symbols and dreams.'

Technological influence may exceed that of surrealism, abstraction, conceptualism. Indeed, part of television's insidious impact is that it actually combines in popularism elements of all three: the expansion and contraction of space and the presentation of familiar objects in irrational aspects, the camera acting, for the benefit of a TV commercial, as the *surreal* imagination; the sensibility to *abstraction* stimulated by a speeded-up succession of images that blur the figurative into a swirl of light, colour, and line; the *conceptual* choice the images of television make in material by the medium's necessity to present ideas in iconography. I know that every workshop of young painters in my country shows strikingly the imprinting of artists' creativity by television's imagery, television's *visual hierarchy of what is meaningful in our life*.

I am not forgetting that television is the luxuriant twentieth-century spawn of the aptly-named Lumière brothers, who invented cinematic art which democratized the enjoyment of leisure before television entered homes; founded an important industry in a number of countries; created a new pantheon of performer-gods and -goddesses in a new, substitute, religion of success-worship world-wide, and also proved itself a new medium for great creativity in the work of directors like Eisenstein, Buñuel, Fellini, Bergman, Satyajit Ray, Kurosawa.

The fact is, television has empowered the visual far beyond the capacity of the cinema. Through this service of technology to art, developed in our century, we have produced a human mutation, a species that substitutes vicarious experience for the real thing.

'One of the things a writer is for is to say the unsayable, to speak the unspeakable, to ask difficult questions.'

So writes Salman Rushdie, one of the interpreters of the real thing, while living through the most recent of its traumas; defining a credo for us.

Tolstoy, Dostoevsky, Turgenev, Ibsen began the century with questions we expected Marx and Freud to answer. Proust, Joyce, Kafka, followed by Lawrence, Genet, Mishima, spoke the unspeakable (the names in all categories are representative, not inclusive). Kafka was the one who went furthest, presaging in his story-telling genius what grim history had in store— fascism, Nazism, dictatorship. (Did he miss the return of the religious inquisition in a twentieth-century avatar? I have to reread him yet again . . .)

With Thomas Mann's intuition of politics as the meaning of destiny in our time, literature's position as both a deeper and higher understanding of human striving than that in which politics operates, changes: literature becomes inexorably a medium through which that political operation is expressed at a deeper and higher level. If destiny is political, politics and liter-ature cannot be kept hierarchically apart.

Would Bertolt Brecht have known that 'to speak of trees is almost a crime/For it is a kind of silence about injustice' if he had not formed his creative consciousness in the years of Hitler's creation, Nazism, and in the imperative of resistance to this fate?

Would 1916 have the resonance, in the history of our era, without Yeats's poem of that date whose line 'a terrible beauty is born' rings on down our years, tolling the awesome pain and exal-tation of disparate struggles for freedom. You heard it in India, you heard it, on and on, in Cuba, in Vietnam, in South Africa.

I can speak of literature and politics, pass from one to the other in one breath, so to say, because the former—literature—is created inescapably *within* the destined context of politics. Even literary style, which Proust defines as 'the moment of identifica-

tion between the author and his subject', is also the identification between the author and this destined political context.

. We are not only children of our time but of our place. My
own consciousness and subconscious, from which I write, come
even in the most personal aspects of mind and spirit from destiny shaped by the historico-political matrix into which I was
born. The unspeakable shame and horror of the Holocaust and
Hiroshima: this heading to our century stands. Beside it, my
personal sense of the defining events of our century is dominated
by two: the fall of Communism, and the end of colonialism. And
the two extraordinary developments are linked subjectively,
even contradictorily, for me, since I was born a second-genera-
tion colonial in a capitalist-racist society and as I grew up I
looked to the Left as the solution to the oppression of the poor
and powerless all around me, in my home country and the world.

Satyajit Ray the Indian film-maker and writer has said, 'It is
the presence of the essential thing in a very small detail which
one must catch in order to expose larger things.'

This principle I believe applies beyond art, to the general
level of awareness of your world with which you were presented
when you opened your eyes. The essential detail that exposes the
larger things in my life begins very early. I was taken as a toddler
to wave a flag at the Prince of Wales, the future Edward VIII, on
his imperial visit to the then British Dominion, South Africa. As
I grew, I was told again and again of this momentous occasion,
with a sense of values to be inculcated: loyalty in homage to
imperial power, white man's power.

Nobody presented for the formation of my sense of values
the fact that Mohandas Gandhi had lived in and developed his
philosophy in and through the country where I was born and
was to live my life; the man who was to leave behind in that
country principles of liberation that were to be fundamental to

the struggle for freedom by the black people, my brothers and sisters unacknowledged by the values of the whites who took me to make obeisance to an English prince. The essence of the colonial ethos in which I was brought up is contained in a detail: the flag I was given to wave.

South Africa raised an army to fight Nazism, which it did with distinction; and the same brave white men and women under the command of Prime Minister General Smuts came back to practise racism contentedly at home. In that war, South Africa had suffered neither invasion nor bombardment, but there was a shortage of nurses. As a seventeen-year-old Red Cross recruit, I was sent to a first-aid station at a gold mine in the town where I lived. There I saw the mine's white Medical Aid worker stitch, without anaesthetic, the gaping wounds black miners had suffered from falling rock underground. He grinned and told me: 'They don't feel like we do.'

Not the shootings at Sharpeville in 1960, the deaths in prison by torture and neglect, of Steve Biko and nameless others, or the herding of people from their homes with guns and dogs at their heels in the mass removals of black populations off land whites coveted, in the sixties and seventies, epitomise racism, for me, as does that single utterance at the mine.

It has become a truism to shake one's head in wonder at the end of apartheid and the emergence of a free South Africa the twentieth century has just seen.

A miracle; and coming to pass at the time when a new miracle is yearningly needed to compensate for the miracle the first quarter of the century promised—now a fallen star, the red star, flickered out.

Human beings will always have the imperative to believe in the possibility of a better world of their own making. In the words of one of the most influential thinkers of the mid-century, Jean-Paul Sartre, socialism was 'man in the process of creating himself.' The end of the human's identity as a beast of burden on the dreadful journey from feudal slavery through wage slavery. The Communist Manifesto, its enactment in the Soviet Union, promised the miracle in what seemed to be the culmination of all the world's revolutionary attempts to end exploitation, poverty, degradation. It was the Red Flag and not the Statue of Liberty that summoned all to bread and justice, when I was young.

The depth of the sense of abandonment, now, not only among those who were Communists but among all of us to whom the Left, the ideals of socialism remain, although these have been betrayed and desecrated in many countries, as well as in the Gulags of the founding one—it is this *sense of abandonment* that the collapse of the Soviet Union brings to our century, rather than the disillusion the West would triumphantly claim.

Whatever one's judgment of its consequences, the most momentous single date in the social organization of our century was unquestionably the October Revolution, as a result of which one-third of humanity found itself living under regimes derived from it. The disintegration of the Soviet world before the end of the same century that saw its beginning: has it brought the triumph of democracy or only the return of the liberalism that failed, after the First World War, to prevent the poor and unemployed of Italy and Germany from turning to fascism as the solution of their circumstances, many of which exist again today?

It is conveniently overlooked that the Soviet Union's communist army, in the Second World War, was definitive in defeating the Nazis; it is the evil you do that lives after you, not the good. Yet the *great positive achievement of our century, the end of colonialism*, that has come to realization in contrast to the tragedy of the Russian attempt to improve our human lot, owes much to the thought crystallized in Marx and Lenin, and cast in different lights by Rosa Luxemburg, Gramsci, Mao Tse-tung, Ho Chi Minh, Fanon—to turn the prism about to reveal only a few of its facets.

This does not apply alone to the colonial 'possessions' that set up declared Marxist-Leninist states when they attained their freedom from colonial powers.

Those who were purely nationalist or ethnic in their concept of freedom from colonial rule also were inspired by the precept of power in the hands of the people—'Freedom for the huts! Wars to the palaces!'—which released them, ready to act, from the spell of overlordship in which governors and commissioners held them convinced of their helplessness. The liberal alleviations on option came from the same countries that had cast the spell over three hundred years of colonisation; little wonder reform was distrusted.

I can affirm that in my own country, South Africa, Communism's revelation of the class and economic basis of the Colour Bar was one of the formative influences that joined the people's natural, inevitable will towards liberation. From the Freedom Charter of 1955 to the Constitution of the new South Africa in 1994, incorporations derived from the best of socialism's provisions for a truly human society can be traced and are being devolved, attempted in practice, in the country's reconstruction and development plans. Perhaps we are not doomed to repeat the mistakes of the past so long as we look at our century critically and have the courage to pick up again and use what was misused but is not invalidated, belongs still to hard-won increment of human advancement.

The other formative influence on the liberation movement in South Africa was one of the truly great individuals of our century whose lifetime within it we set against the monsters the century has produced.

A young Indian lawyer who came to South Africa to defend South African Indians against discriminatory laws became Mahatma Gandhi, an original thinker on *the nature of power*, as distinct from power confined to the purely political Leftist conception as the tool for liberation, yet able to serve this tool as part of a high moral consciousness.

This original thinking is an important component of the intellectual advancement of our century and perhaps the only genuine spiritual advancement in an era of religious decline marked by crack-pot distortions of faith, and, finally, by savage fundamentalism. It was within his South African experience that Gandhi formulated a concept of power that he called Satyagraha, contracted from its linguistic combination, 'satya'—truth, 'agraha'—firmness, which he defined as 'the force which is born of Truth and Love or non-violence'. It was a force he went on to develop in India and which was to bring about India's freedom from British rule.

Mohandas Gandhi's philosophy, which gained freedom for India, became part of the struggle that gained freedom for my own country, South Africa.

'Satyagraha postulates the conquest of the adversary by suffering in one's own person.'

For the South African liberation movement, Gandhi's dictum supplied not only tactics for the non-violent resistance campaigns against the unjust laws of apartheid in the 1950s, it became a text for endurance of the enormous suffering of blacks *in their own person* that was the price of their armed resistance when that phase came, whether in exchange of stones against the agony of police bullets in the townships, or in the heat and thirst of guerrilla battle in the bush.

Apartheid was an avatar of Nazism. The theories of racial superiority and most of the repulsive and cruel ways of implementing them were the same in both regimes, except that instead of being perpetrated on Jews, Gypsies, and homosexuals, in South Africa these were perpetrated on the majority of the population—any, all who were not white-skinned.

Apartheid was also an avatar of fascism, if that means, as Umberto Eco writes, 'a regime that subordinates every act of the individual to the state and its ideology'.

Apartheid contained, concealed within its own evil, these two, which the poverty the First World War brought about by its human devastation, and the Second World War was supposed to have banished by means of *its* human devastation. Apartheid was, finally, the last act in civilisation's shameful saga of colonialism, where, decked out in different guises by the colonial powers and those without colonial possessions who benefited from cheap primary products, the theory of racial superiority and the theory of subordination of every act of the individual to the ideology of state rule, had leading roles.

Nelson Mandela's unmatched, unchallengeable prestige and honour in the world today is recognition not only of his achievement, with and for his people, in defeat of the dire twentieth-century experiment in social engineering called apartheid. It is recognition that other ghastly forms of social engineering tried in our century were defeated where they had taken refuge; finally, it is homage paid to him in recognition that what was at stake was something greater by far than the fate of a single country: it was victory gained for humankind over centuries-old bondage of colonisation.

In the world-wide, immediate context of cataclysmic cracks which have opened with the earthquake of old national conflicts exploding surface solutions once imposed by now defunct political powers of East and West, President Mandela is looked to as the man of the century who, alone of others, knows how to bring about reconciliation between people who regard one another as enemies but must learn to live together.

Yet Mandela, at home, takes up every day the peace-time struggle with aleatory circumstances bequeathed by a former regime: the landless, the workless, the homeless. His ethos is that freedom in democracy must somehow be made real for the people in their daily lives.

The sum of our century may be looked at in a number of ways.

The wars that were fought, the military defeats that turned into economic victories, the ideologies that rose and fell, the technology that telescoped time and distance.

Women's rights have at last been recognized as full *human* rights entrenched in many contemporary constitutions, an emancipation from gender oppression that went back beyond the male dominance enshrined in holy texts of many religions, all the way to club-wielding cave-man.

And there are ironies in our history: such as that of the twentieth-century State of Israel. Driven about the world for two thousand years, Jews returned home to ancient ancestral territory won back from Britain, which had occupied it under that form of colonial oppression known as a mandate, only for the Jewish people to find itself inheriting a colonialist position of an occupying power over another people with ancient ancestral claims to the land, the Palestinians. Israelis and Palestinians have been living through the tragic consequences, both suffering and causing suffering in appalling exchange. And Europe conveniently forgets its basic responsibility for this: the British disposal as they pleased of their spoils-of-war mandate over the lives of the Palestinian people, to salve the conscience of the world's two-thousand-year crimes of vile anti-Semitism against the Jewish people, that culminated in the Holocaust.

Freud and Jung changed self-perception and emotional cognition—furthered the possibility of understanding the mysteries of human behaviour. Another kind of perception moved from Picasso's *Guernica* to a Campbell's Soup can, to the Reichstag wrapped in plastic, illustrating our cycles—worship of force and destruction, worship of materialism, desire to cover up and forget these choices we have made.

But what are the factors that affect those daily lives—ours—running across calendar events, a continuous element of end-of-the-century existence, over trade winds and continents and national frontiers, in which haves and have-nots in the world all live, if far from alike in respect of other circumstances? What influences the late-twentieth-century world most widely, you and me, now?

Dip a finger in a dark viscous substance and write on the window of our world OIL.

There always has been awe of gold, a mythology of gold as the ultimate in material value; gold as the alchemy in which human fate is bound up. At the end of this century it is oil that should have that significance.

Oil is ominously bound up with our time; it was the base of the Nobel fortune from which came the Peace Prize . . . and undreamt-of means of destruction. It is the 'why' of many wars of our day; of the huge profit of sanctions-busters who fuel those wars, in every sense, in defiance of sanctions imposed by international treaties and the efforts of international peace-keeping organizations. Repressive regimes go unreproached by democratic countries who are dependent upon them for oil. The horrors of the Nigerian regime, in this very decade, went virtually uncensured until November 1995. Men, women, and children die, for oil, without knowing it. What lit the lamps and brought our ancestors out of darkness, powered the machines and warmed the homes through modern times—this benefice is our pervasive source of bloody conflict, the low-profile version of the other means of human advancement turned to the service of violence, atomic power.

In human relations, the most intimate form, shared by all, has been transformed for us. We have sexual freedom as never before known to any generation. We have easy means of enjoying sex without conception, democratically available devices for this supplied in vending machines, as for cigarettes or chocolate bars, in the streets of many cities.

We even have routine means of creating conception, if we wish, in laboratories, when couples desire children and cannot achieve this in their own sexual relations.

Homoerotic and lesbian relations are widely tolerated as a right of choice and non-discrimination, if disapproved of by many people. Condemning edicts of certain religious leaders are contested by some of their own followers, just as the edicts against birth control are ignored by them. Abortion, regarded as the democratic right of women to control of their bodies, is contested by many groups on the premise of the right to life of the unborn, but abortion is no longer a taboo subject locked away in the secret which sex used to be.

Yet with sexual freedom granted by Freud, by law, by medical discoveries, we now have the ultimate inhibition: death through sex. AIDS. An incurable disease. Acquired Immune Deficiency Syndrome. How did we acquire it? Is it something for which we have no behavioural responsibility? A mutation in that swarming soup of lower life-forms in which we have our existence, but over which we have no control? Something which we then host helplessly in our flesh and blood? Or is it something we have done, brought upon ourselves in the way we have lived?

Inevitably, there are some who see it in moral terms, not only the direct ones of sexual promiscuity (and no-one can say for certain that we have become more promiscuous than previous generations, since perhaps we are just more open to scrutiny on the subject). Have we perhaps abused our other but contingent freedoms—moving about the world taking as our right disregard for the social and sexual mores of other races and peoples, seeing concourse across borders and classes not as an exchange of cultures but as a sweeping aside of these, since differences are most easily dealt with by dissolving them in respect for nothing, none, neither yours nor mine?

Have we assumed to *act without consequences*, whether trampling monuments or seducing, become mercenaries of moral exploitation disguised as freedom—drive off, hop on the next plane, no care for what you have broken or what, broken in yourself, you take away.

It is human, if primitive, to have an inkling fear that we are somewhere to blame. If medical science is to lift the death sentence of AIDS, shall we in some way be responsible to ensure, in the whole context of our morals and mores, that it shall not reinstate itself?

In what men and women cannot deal with, they traditionally resort to God; I use the singular conveniently for *the gods*, the forms in which highest being is conceived by different faiths.

This resort is surely problematic in the sum of our century. In its mid-decades, the intellectuals of the Western world, particularly France, announced that God was dead. Life had long ceased to be a performance before the judgment of the gods, as it had been in antiquity and later centuries, and we were performing only for ourselves, in lack of faith, without hope of the grace of higher judgment.

This was a Eurocentric, Judeo-Christian point of view; certainly ignored the continued existence, in faith, of the gods worshipped in the religions of the largest section of the world's population, the gods of Buddhism, Hinduism, Islam, and others. Indeed, in the 1960s the young people of the West turned to look for God elsewhere, sought some spiritual authority in so-called conversions to Buddhism whose inspirational comfort was more stylish than ontological, a travesty of the real faith itself.

But it is true that in the nineties the churches of the Christian establishment are often empty; I'm told that in Britain some are being utilised as concert halls for classical music instead of sermons and prayers. Even in Catholic countries the congregations are mainly old women, except for the extravaganzas of the Pope in St. Peter's in Rome. There seems to be a revival of observance even among liberal-minded Jews, on the evidence of my own country, South Africa; and political change, freedom to gather in common secular purpose where the church was the sole haven under apartheid, has not diminished the high attendance of black South Africans at the churches of many denominations and sects.

Yet in the Judeo-Christian world religion does appear to have a decisive place in sects alone, as an aspect of conservatism: the revived ancient fundamentalism of ultra-orthodox Jews and the new fundamentalism of Born-again Christians in the United States of America, while some African nationalists rally ancestral beliefs against the betrayals by Christianity they have experienced.

It is no break with the history of religion that people of different faiths engage in violent fundamentalist conflict with one another for political as well as religious reasons.

But in the final quarter of our century religious fundamentalism has joined forces with political terrorism in an unprecedented way, taken up terrorist tactics of pursuing its ends anywhere and everywhere, a law unto itself, an international threat to peace and life on street corners, on aircraft, even in schools, far from its country or countries of origin. Muslim fundamentalism, the distortion of a great religion by fanatics aberrant within its hierarchy, incited further by the power-hungry, conducts a campaign that stalks the world. It seeks to sabotage the historical human necessity of initiatives for territorial justice and coexistence between Israel and Palestine—and, again ironically, is to great extent reinforced in this by Jewish fundamentalists. It declares the *fatwa* of death to Muslim writers and academic scholars branded as heretics wherever they may be, and threatens the existence or establishment of democratic secular freedom in a growing number of countries.

The sum of our century includes the looming of a new Inquisition, not, this time, in the name of Christianity.

Our century has been 'without doubt the most murderous century of which we have record, both by the scale, frequency and length of the warfare which filled it, barely ceasing for a moment in the 1920s, but also by the unparalleled scale, frequency and length of the human catastrophes it produced, from the greatest famines in history to systematic genocide.'

I quote here one better able to judge objectively, perhaps, than I—an eminent historian, Eric Hobsbawm.

It is also the century in which greater technological advance and greater knowledge of human intelligence have taken place in a shorter span than any other century. The conclusion—and our existential conclusion as creatures of our time—is that humankind has not known how to control the marvels of its achievements. What was written in prison by the great leader and thinker, Jawaharlal Nehru, remains for us. He defined this as 'the problems of individual and social life, of harmonious living, of a proper balancing of an individual's inner and outer life, of an adjustment of the relation between individuals and groups, of a continuous becoming something better and higher, of social development, of the *ceaseless adventure of man.*'

Now that the deeds are done, the hundred years ready to seal what will be recorded of us, our last achievement could be in the spirit of taking up, in 'the ceaseless adventure of man', control of our achievements, questioning honestly and reflecting upon the truth of what has been lived through, what has been done. There is no other base on which to found the twenty-first century with any chance to make it a better one.

—*Jawaharlal Nehru Memorial Lecture, 1995*

NOTES

THREE IN A BED: FICTION, MORALS, AND POLITICS

[4] *'The whale is the agent . . . '* Harry Levin, 'The Jonah Complex', *The Power of Blackness* (Vintage Books, 1960), p. 215.

[7] *'My book is going to sell . . . '* *Letters of Gustave Flaubert 1830–1857*, selected, edited and trans. by Francis Steegmuller (Belknap Press, Harvard, 1990), p. 224.

[8] *'undirected play . . . '* Seamus Heaney, *The Government of the Tongue* (Faber & Faber, 1988), p. 96.

[9] *'as not having to do . . . '* From a quote in my notebooks, source not noted.

[9] *'Russia became a garden . . . '* Bely quoted by Peter Levi in *Boris Pasternak* (Hutchinson, 1990), p. 142.

[9] *'We want the glorious . . . '* Quoted by Evgeny Pasternak, *Boris Pasternak: The Tragic Years 1930–60* (Collins Harvill, 1990), p. 38.

[10] *'A sincere but perverted . . . '* Claudio Magris, *Inferences from a Sabre*, trans. Mark Thompson (Polygon, 1990).

[10] *'I told him My Sister, Life . . . '* Quoted by Peter Levi in *Boris Pasternak* (Hutchinson, 1990), p. 100.

[11] *'The lie is quite as real . . . '* Magris, *Inferences*, p. 43.

[11] *'We page through . . . '* Mongane Wally Serote, *A Tough Tale* (Kliptown Books, 1987), p. 7.

[11] *'We want the world . . . '* Ibid.

[12] *'a disease at the very centre . . . '* Harold Pinter, broadcast on Britain's Channel 4 programme *Opinion*, May 31, 1990.

[14] *'guerrillas of the imagination . . . '* Seamus Heaney, 'Osip and Nadezhda Mandelstam', *The Government of the Tongue*, p. 73.

[15] *'help people . . . '* Per Wästberg, addressing PEN International Writers' Day, June 2, 1990.

[15] *'When seats are assigned . . . '* Quoted by Peter Levi in *Boris Pasternak*, p. 159.

THE STATUS OF THE WRITER IN THE WORLD TODAY: WHICH WORLD? WHOSE WORLD?

[19] *they show both the writer and his or her people* what they are . . . Paraphrased by Vladimir Nabokov in *Nikolai Gogol* (New Directions, 1961), p. 129.

[20] *the first congress . . .* Congress of African Writers and Artists, the Sorbonne, Paris, under the auspices of *Présence Africaine*, 1956.

[25] *'imaginary history . . . '* Lebona Mosia, 'Time to Be Truly Part of Africa', *The Star*, Johannesburg, September 26, 1997.

[28] *With the exceptions of the pre-Hispanic civilisations . . .* Octavio Paz, *In Light of India*, trans. Eliot Weinberger (Harcourt Brace, 1997).

[28] *'Every civilisation . . . '* Henri Lopès, *Le Lys et le Flamboyant* (Editions du Seuil, 1997). My translation from the French.

[29] *'What you expect . . . '* Amu Djoleto, 'A Passing Thought', *Messages: Poems from Ghana*, ed. Kofi Awoonor and Adali-Mortty (African Writers Series, 1971).

REFERENCES: THE CODES OF CULTURE

[39] *'to make the reader . . . '* S/Z, trans. Richard Miller, (Farrar, Straus and Giroux, 1974).

[39] *As Richard Howard sums up . . .* 'A Note on S/Z', preface to S/Z by Roland Barthes, p. X1.

[40] *'To survey his writings . . . '* Harry Levin, 'From Obsession to Imagination: The Psychology of the Writer', *Michigan Quarterly Review* X11:3 (Summer 1974), p. 90.

[40] *to survey his . . .* Harry Levin, 'From Obsession to Imagination', p. 90.

[40] *to make the reader . . .* Barthes, *S/Z*, p. 21.

[40] *'Words are symbols . . . '* Jorge Luis Borges, 'The Congress', *The Book of Sand*, trans. Norman Thomas di Giovanni (Penguin, 1979), p. 33.

[42] *Italo Calvino wrote . . .* 'Whom Do We Write For?', *The Literature Machine*, trans. Patrick Creagh (Secker & Warburg, 1987), p. 86.

[45] *'another body of knowledge . . . '* John Berger, 'An Explanation', *Pig Earth* (Pantheon, 1980), p. 9.

[45] *'She writes the kind of fiction . . . '* Lorrie Moore, review of Bobbie Ann Mason's *Love Life* in *The New York Times Book Review*, March 12, 1989.

[45] *there has been demonstrated recently . . .* 1996 census records population as 40,583,573, of whom 4,434,697 are white. An officially unconfirmed census in 1998 gives a figure of 46 million.

THE LION, THE BULL, AND THE TREE

[50] *'The African Apprehension of Reality'*, from *Senghor: Prose and Poetry*, ed. John Reed and Clive Wake (Heinemann, 1976).

[52] *'Lord God, forgive . . . '* Ibid.

[52] *As Claude Wauthier remarks . . . The Literature and Thought of Modern Africa* (Pall Mall Library of African Affairs, 1966).

[53] *'Senghor sees Chaka . . . '* Ibid.

[54] *'unity is rediscovered . . . '* 'New York', *Senghor: Prose and Poetry*.

THE DIALOGUE OF LATE AFTERNOON

[59] *the latest work . . .* Naguib Mahfouz, *Echoes of an Autobiography* (Anchor Books, 1997).

[60] *he has the gift . . .* 'Zaabalawi: The Concealed Side', Nadine Gordimer, *Writing and Being* (Harvard University Press, 1995).

[65] *'Zaabalawi', The Time and the Place, and Other Stories* (Doubleday, 1991).

JOSEPH ROTH: LABYRINTH OF EMPIRE AND EXILE

[69] 'Je travaille, . . . ' In a letter to his translator, Blanche Gidon, quoted by Beatrice Musgrave in her introduction to *Weights and Measures* (Everyman's Library, 1983), p. 9. Roth lived in Paris for some years and two of his novels, *Le Triomphe de la Beauté* and *Le Buste de L'Empereur*, were published first in French, not German. *Le Triomphe de la Beauté* probably was written in French; it appears not to have been published in German.

[70] '*One can't be angry* . . . ' Robert Musil, *The Man Without Qualities*, trans. Eithne Wilkins and Ernst Kaiser (Secker & Warburg, 1961). Musil was born in 1880, and though long neglected, he was not forgotten as long as Roth. Musil became a figure in world literature in the fifties; Roth's work had to wait another twenty years before being reissued in Germany, let alone in translation. A new and more complete translation of Musil's novel, by Sophie Wilkins and Burton Pike, was published in 1995.

[70] *(1928?) The Silent Prophet* was put together from unpublished work, with the exception of fragments published in *24 Neue Deutsche Erzähler* and *Die Neue Rundschau* in 1929, and was published long after Roth's death, in 1966. The work appears to have been written, with interruptions, over several years. The central character, Kargan, is supposedly modelled on Trotsky.

[70] '*Found unfit* . . . ' Joseph Roth, *The Emperor's Tomb* (Chatto & Windus), p. 119.

[71] '*We love the world* . . . ' Roth, *Right and Left* (Chatto & Windus), p. 48.

[72] '*intended to exemplify* . . . ' Roth, *The Silent Prophet* (The Overlook Press), p. 9.

[73] '*Ill at ease* . . . ' Czeslaw Milosz, 'To Raja Rao', *Selected Poems* (The Ecco Press, 1980), p. 29.

[74] *the dating of his novels* . . . The dates I cite are generally the dates of first publication in the original German.

[75] '*fall into a gloomy* . . . ' Roth, *Right and Left*.

[75] '*It seemed to the stationmaster* . . . ' *Fallmerayer the Stationmaster,* in *Hotel Savoy,* which also includes 'The Bust of the Emperor' (Chatto & Windus), p. 131.

[76] '*Though fate elected him* . . . ' Roth, *The Radetzky March* (The Overlook Press/Tusk).

[78] '*This is for you, Herr Baron* . . . ' Roth, *The Emperor's Tomb* (Chatto & Windus).

[80] *'an extensiveness . . . '* Walter Benjamin, 'One-Way Street', *Reflections: Essays, Aphorisms, Autobiographical Writings*, ed. Peter Dementz, trans. Edmund Jephcott (Schocken Books).

[80] *'Lieutenant Trotta died . . . '* *The Radetzsky March*, p. 309.

[81] *'My friends' excitement . . . Long live the Emperor'*, *The Emperor's Tomb*, p. 152–56.

[102] 'History says . . . ' Seamus Heaney, *The Cure at Troy* (Farrar, Straus and Giroux, 1991).

HOW SHALL WE LOOK AT EACH OTHER THEN?

[139] *'So we shall have buried apartheid . . . '* Mongane Wally Serote, *A Tough Tale*, p. 7.

[139] *an American analyst of world problems* . . . Flora Lewis, International *Herald Tribune*, June 20, 1990.

[141] *Sixty-six*. According to Major-General Herman Stadler, the South African Police expert on 'terror' organizations, sixty-one whites have been killed in Freedom Fighter (he terms them terrorist) attacks since 1976. Information supplied to Allister Sparks, August 23, 1990. According to Mr Sparks' files, there were five other deaths of this nature between 1960 and 1976, bringing the total to sixty-six by August 1990.

[143] *'If we want things . . . '* Giuseppe di Lampedusa, *The Leopard*, trans. Archibald Colquhoun (London: Collins Harvill, 1960), p. 31.

[144] *Václav Havel said* . . . From my notes, taken at a conference, 'The Anatomy of Hate—Resolving Conflict Through Dialogue and Democracy', Oslo, August 1990.

ACT TWO: ONE YEAR LATER

[170] *I quote Leibniz's gibe . . . Philosophische Schriften von G. W. Leibniz*, ed. C. I. Gerhardt (Berlin, 1875–90), Vol. IV, p. 329. Leibniz's statement, like Descartes' Rule, is quoted from Bernard Williams's study *Descartes: The Project of Pure Enquiry* (Pelican Books, 1978), p. 32.

AS OTHERS SEE US

[177] *'Tough Love Crowd'* . . .   Ronald Suresh Roberts, *Clarence Thomas: Tough Love Crowd; Counterfeit Heroes and Unhappy Truths* (New York University Press, 1995).

LABOUR WELL THE TEEMING EARTH

[185] *'might do well to re-dedicate themselves* . . . ' Pranay Gupta, International *Herald Tribune*, September 16, 1997.

THE WRITER'S IMAGINATION AND THE IMAGINATION OF THE STATE

[192] *what Lukács calls* . . . *Theory of the Novel*.
[194] *'to discover the conditions* . . . ' 'What Is Epic Theatre'. From *Illuminations*, trans. Harry Zohn (Fontana, 1983).

WRITING AND BEING

[196] *Like the prisoner* . . . Jorge Luis Borges, 'The God's Script', *Labyrinths and Other Writings*, ed. Donald H. Yates and James E. Irby. (Penguin, 1988).
[197] *Roland Barthes asks* . . . *Mythologies*, trans. Annette Lavers (Hill and Wang), p. 131.
[197] *Claude Lévi-Strauss wittily de-mythologizes* . . . ' . . . je les situais à mi-chemin entre le conte de fées et le roman policier', *Histoire de Lynx* (Plon), p. 13.
[197] *as Nikos Kazantzakis once wrote* . . . *Report to Greco* (Faber & Faber), p. 150.
[198] *as Roland Barthes does* . . . *S/Z*.
[199] *Anthony Burgess once gave* . . . London *Observer*, April 19, 1981.
[200] *a little Kafka parable* . . . Franz Kafka, 'The Third Octavo Notebook', *Wedding Preparations in the Country* (Secker & Warburg).

[202] *Camus dealt* . . . Albert Camus, *Carnets 1942–5*.

[202] *And Márquez redefined* tendenz *fiction thus* . . . Gabriel García Márquez, in an interview. My notes do not give the journal or date.

[203] *Czeslaw Milosz once wrote* . . . 'Dedication', *Selected Poems* (The Ecco Press).

[203] *and Brecht wrote* . . . 'To Posterity', *Selected Poems of Bertolt Brecht*, trans. H. R. Hays (Grove Press), p. 173.

[203] *'make the decision* . . . ' Nikos Kazantzakis, *Report to Greco*.

LIVING ON A FRONTIERLESS LAND: CULTURAL GLOBALIZATION

[210] *Edward Said cites* . . . *Orientalism* (Vintage Books, 1979), p. 25.

[213] *Claude Lévi-Strauss's splendid exegesis* . . . *The Raw and the Cooked: Introduction to a Science of Mythology*, Vol. 1 (Jonathan Cape, 1970).

OUR CENTURY

[216] *'If I cannot move Heaven* . . . ' Virgil's lines from the *Aeneid*, as translated by Freud as a motto for his *Interpretation of Dreams*.

[216] *'the defining moments of terror* . . . ' Gar Alperovitz, 'The Truman Show', *Los Angeles Times Book Review*, August 9, 1998.

[216] *'are not merely* . . . ' *The Crazy Iris, and Other Stories of the Atomic Aftermath*, ed. Kenzaburo Oe (Grove Press, 1985).

[217] France was followed by India and Pakistan in 1998.

[223] *'One of the things* . . . ' Salman Rushdie in an interview, London, 1995.

[224] *'to speak of trees* . . . ' 'To Posterity', *Selected Poems of Bertolt Brecht*, trans. H. R. Hays (Grove Press, 1959).

[224] *'a terrible beauty is born'* . . . 'Easter 1916', *Collected Poems of W. B. Yeats* (Macmillan, 1950).

[224] *which Proust defines* . . . Quoted by Robert Painter in *Marcel Proust*, Vol. 11, p. 307.

[225] *Satyajit Ray, Indian film-maker* . . . Quoted by Andrew Robinson in 'The Inner Eye: Aspects of Satyajit Ray', *London*, October, 1982.

[226] *'man in the process . . . '* Sartre, *Le Fantôme de Staline*. (Publisher not recorded in my notebooks.)

[228] *'Freedom for the huts! . . . '* Georg Büchner, *Der Hessische Landbote* (The Hessian Messenger). (Publisher not recorded in my notebooks.)

[229] *Gandhi formulated a concept* . . . M. K. Gandhi, *Satyagraha in South Africa* (Ahmedabad: Navajivan Publishing House, 1950).

[229] *'Satyagraha postulates . . . '* Ibid.

[230] *as Umberto Eco writes* . . . 'Ur-Fascism', *The New York Review of Books*, June 22, 1995.

[236] *'without doubt the most murderous . . . '* Eric Hobsbawm, *The Age of Extremes: The Short 20th Century 1914–1918* (Michael Joseph), p. 13.

[236] *'ceaseless adventure of man . . . '* Jawaharlal Nehru, *The Discovery of India* (Meridian Books, 1951), p. 16.

A NOTE ON THE AUTHOR

Nadine Gordimer's many novels include *The Lying Days* (her first novel), *The Conservationist*, joint winner of the Booker Prize, *Burger's Daughter, July's People, My Son's Story, None to Accompany Me*, and most recently, *The House Gun*. Her collections of short stories include *Something Out There* and *Jump*. In 1991 she was awarded the Nobel Prize for Literature. She lives in South Africa.